Got it!

Level 1
Student Book & Workbook

Philippa Bowen & Denis Delaney

OXFORD
UNIVERSITY PRESS

Contents

Communication	Skills
Making requests **Pronunciation:** Rising intonation in questions and falling intonation in answers	**Reading:** A magazine article about basketball coaches **Listening:** A phone call about a summer camp **Speaking:** A conversation a summer camp **Writing:** A postcard about a summer camp
Agreeing and disagreeing **Pronunciation:** Sentence stress	**Reading:** A biography of Bono **Listening:** A biography of Elvis Presley **Speaking:** Factfiles of Justin Timberlake and Shakira **Writing:** A personal profile of your favorite pop singer

Curriculum extra A, Music: pages C1–C2

Communication	Skills
Apologizing and making excuses **Pronunciation:** /ɑ/ and /oʊ/	**Reading:** A biography of Christopher Columbus **Listening:** A biography of George Washington **Speaking:** A presentation of the life of William Shakespeare or Marie Curie **Writing:** An description of the life of William Shakespeare or Marie Curie
Buying a movie ticket **Pronunciation:** /s/, /k/, and /tʃ/	**Reading:** An interview with Shia LaBeouf **Listening:** A conversation about a movie **Speaking:** Discussing a movie **Writing:** A description of two movies

Curriculum extra B, Media studies: pages C3–C4

Communication	Skills
Making arrangements **Pronunciation:** /oʊ/ and /u/	**Reading:** A magazine article about skateboarding across Australia **Listening:** An interview with a skateboarder **Speaking:** A trip to San Diego **Writing:** An e-mail about a trip
Ordering food and drink **Pronunciation:** *would you*	**Reading:** A magazine article about a teen celebrity chef. **Listening:** Two teenagers talking about their diets **Speaking:** A food survey **Writing:** Your diet

Curriculum extra C, Citizenship: pages C5–C6

Communication	Skills
Asking for tourist information **Pronunciation:** /ə/	**Reading:** A magazine article about bizarre pets **Listening:** Giving advice about guinea pigs and hamsters **Speaking:** Talking about your favorite animals **Writing:** The differences between traditional and exotic pets
Making a phone call **Pronunciation:** /h/	**Reading:** A magazine article about colors **Listening:** Teenagers talking about their favorite colors **Speaking:** Talking about your favorite colors **Writing:** A text about your favorite colors

Curriculum extra D, Geography: pages C7–C8

Welcome

Vocabulary
Countries and nationalities

1 Match the countries with the flags. Then write the nationalities.

~~Brazil~~ Canada Japan South Korea
the United Kingdom the United States

Brazil   1 _____   2 _____   3 _____   4 _____   5 _____
Brazilian   _____   _____   _____   _____   _____

Family

2 Look at Ella's family tree. Complete the sentences.

Ralph is the children's <u>grandpa</u>.
1 Sue is Tim's _____.
2 Sara is Matthew's _____.
3 Laura is Matthew and Luisa's _____.
4 Matthew is Ella's _____.
5 Thomas is Ella and Luisa's _____.
6 Ralph is Tim's _____.
7 Ella is Luisa's _____.
8 Sara is Thomas's _____.
9 Tim is Ella's _____.
10 Ralph and Laura are Luisa's _____.

Ralph — Laura

Sara — Tim   Sue — Kevin

Matthew   Ella   Luisa   Thomas

Daily routines and free-time activities

3 Complete the text. Use the pictures to help you.

My favorite day is Saturday. I <u>get up</u>  at 10 o'clock. Then I ¹ _____

 with Mom and we ² _____  downtown. In the

afternoon, I usually ³ _____  or I ⁴ _____

and in the evening, I sometimes ⁵ _____  with my friends. I always

⁶ _____  late!

House and furniture

4 Write the names of the rooms in the house (A–E). Then write the furniture (1–8).

A _bedroom_   1 _bed_
B _____   2 _____
C _____   3 _____
D _____   4 _____
E _____   5 _____
                  6 _____
                  7 _____
                  8 _____

Sports

5 Look at the pictures and complete the crossword. What is the mystery sport?

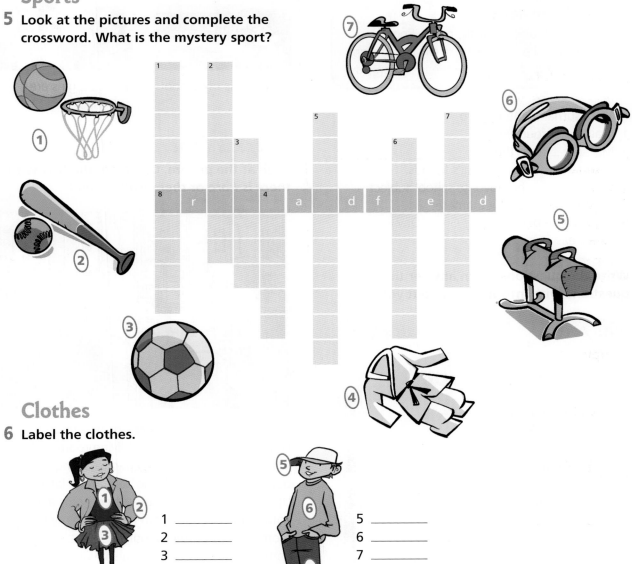

Clothes

6 Label the clothes.

1 _____   5 _____
2 _____   6 _____
3 _____   7 _____
4 _____   8 _____

7 What are you wearing? Complete the sentence.

I'm wearing …

Grammar
be: Simple present

1 Read the factfile. Then complete the sentences about Mai. Use the affirmative or negative form of the verb *be*.

> **Factfile**
> Name: Mai Motegi
> Age: 14
> Country: Vietnam
> School: International School of Hanoi, 10th grade
> Favorite subjects: music, math, English
> Friends: Luke (American), Kelly (Australian)
> Favorite band: Black Eyed Peas, Green Day

Mai's surname <u>isn't</u> Naito.
1 Mai _____ fourteen.
2 Mai _____ from the U.S.
3 Luke and Kelly _____ Mai's friends.
4 Science _____ her favorite school subject.
5 Her friends _____ Vietnamese.
6 Her favorite bands _____ Green Day and Black Eyed Peas.

2 Write the questions. Then answer the questions with information about you.

Who are you?

What / your name?
My name's ...
_____

1 How old / you?
_____

2 you / from Brazil?
_____

3 music / your favorite subject?
_____

4 Who / your friends?
_____

5 Green Day / your favorite band?
_____

Demonstratives: *this, that, these, those*

3 Complete the sentences with *this*, *that*, *these*, and *those*.

1 _____ are my parents, Sara and Tim.

2 _____ is my cat, Sasha.

3 _____ is my school.

4 _____ girls are Canadian.

There is (There's) / There are

4 Look at the picture. Complete the text with *there is / are* or *there isn't / aren't*.

My house is big and <u>there are</u> two floors. Downstairs, ¹_____ a living room and a kitchen. ²_____ a separate dining room, but ³_____ a dining area in the kitchen. Upstairs, ⁴_____ three bedrooms and a bathroom. The bathroom is between my parents' room and my brother's room. ⁵_____ a bathtub, but ⁶_____ a shower, a sink, and a toilet. My bedroom is big. It's my sister's bedroom, too. ⁷_____ two beds, two desks, and two wardrobes. ⁸_____ any posters on the wall, but ⁹_____ a mirror.

Simple present

5 **Write the questions. Then answer the questions.**

Tony / get up at 7 a.m. (?)
He / get up at 7:30 a.m. (✓)
Does Tony get up at 7 a.m?
No, he doesn't. / He doesn't get up at 7 a.m.
He gets up at 7:30 a.m.

1 Jenny / have breakfast in the kitchen (**?**)
  She / have breakfast in the living room (✓)
2 Larry and Walter / play baseball (**?**)
  They / play basketball (✓)
3 Ethan / play the guitar (**?**)
  He / play the piano (✓)
4 Tom and Laura / live in a small house (**?**)
  They / live in a big house (✓)
5 The show / start at 8 o'clock. (**?**)
  It / start at 8:30. (✓)

6 **Complete the e-mail with the correct form of the verbs.**

Hi! My name's Melissa. I _live_ (live) in Seattle, Washington. I ¹_____ (go) to Hamilton Junior High School.
I ²_____ (get up) at 7 o'clock. I ³_____ (have) breakfast with my family. My mom is a teacher at my school. She ⁴_____ (teach) P.E. School ⁵_____ (start) at 8:45 and it ⁶_____ (finish) at 3 o'clock.
I ⁷_____ (get) home at around 3:30.
I usually ⁸_____ (watch) TV for an hour, and then I ⁹_____ (do) my homework.
Dad ¹⁰_____ (get) home from work at 6:30 and then we ¹¹_____ (have) dinner.
I ¹²_____ (not / go) out with my friends on school days.
After dinner, I ¹³_____ (listen) to music or I ¹⁴_____ (chat) with my friends on the Internet. I ¹⁵_____ (go) to bed at 10:30.
Where ¹⁶_____ (you / go) to school? What ¹⁷_____ (you / do) in your free time?

7 **Write questions about Melissa. Then answer the questions.**

Where / she / live?
Where does she live?
She lives in Seattle, Washington.

1 Where / she / go to school?
2 Who / she / have breakfast with?
3 What / her mom / teach?
4 What time / school / start?
5 What / she / do / before dinner?
6 What / Melissa and her friends / do after dinner?

Adverbs of frequency

8 **Put the adverbs of frequency into the correct order.**

~~always~~   ~~never~~   often   rarely
sometimes   usually

<u>always</u>	● ● ● ● ●
1 _____	● ● ● ● ○
2 _____	● ● ● ○ ○
3 _____	● ● ○ ○ ○
4 _____	● ○ ○ ○ ○
<u>never</u>	○ ○ ○ ○ ○

9 **Rewrite the sentences with the correct adverbs of frequency.**

We play soccer in the park. (● ● ○ ○ ○)
We sometimes play soccer in the park.

1 Paula takes a shower before breakfast.
  (● ● ● ● ●)
2 Our teacher is late for class. (○ ○ ○ ○ ○)
3 Ken gets up at 8 a.m. (● ● ● ○ ○)
4 They go to bed before 10 p.m. (● ○ ○ ○ ○)
5 I go cycling with my dad. (● ● ● ● ○)
6 He's happy. (● ● ● ○ ○)

How often ...?

10 Look at Helen's schedule. Ask and answer questions about how often she does things.

How often / watch *House*?
How often does Helen watch "House"?
She watches "House" twice a week.

1 How often / watch TV?
_____

2 How often / go to the sports center with Kelly?
_____

3 How often / have pizza with her friends?
_____

4 How often / visit her grandma?
_____

5 How often / go shopping with her mom?
_____

Sunday:	get up at 9:30 a.m.
	watch TV
Monday:	go to the sports center with Kelly
	watch *House* on TV
Tuesday:	go to a dance lesson with Tracy
	visit grandma
Wednesday:	go to the sports center with Kelly
	watch *Ugly Betty* on TV
Thursday:	go to the movies with Susan
	have pizza with friends
Friday:	go to the sports center with Kelly
	watch *House* on TV
Saturday:	go shopping with mom
	visit grandma

can (ability)

11 Look at the pictures. Write questions and answers about what the people *can* and *can't* do.

Katie
Can Katie sing?
Yes, she can. She can sing,
but she can't dance.

1 Robbie
_____
_____
_____

2 The children
_____
_____
_____

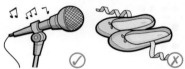

3 Olivia
_____
_____
_____

4 Mark
_____
_____
_____

5 My little brother
_____
_____
_____

Imperatives

12 Complete the school rules with the affirmative or negative imperative forms of the verbs in the box.

be ~~be~~   eat   leave   stand up
use   walk   ~~wear~~

Hardwick High School Rules

1 <u>Don't wear</u> jeans. (✗)
2 <u>Be</u> on time for class. (✓)
3 _____ cell phones. (✗)
4 _____ or drink during class. (✗)
5 _____ when a teacher enters the classroom. (✓)
6 _____. Don't run! (✓)
7 _____ the school at lunch time. (✗)

Present progressive

13 **Look at the picture of the party. What are teenagers (1–5) doing?**

1 She's *taking a photo*.
2 They_____.
3 She_____.
4 They_____.
5 They_____.

14 **The sentences about teenagers (6–10) are incorrect. Correct them.**

6 They're looking at a book.
They aren't looking at a book.
They're watching TV.

7 He's doing homework.
_____

8 He's writing an e-mail.
_____

9 She's dancing.
_____

10 She's playing chess.
_____

15 **Write the questions. Then answer the questions.**

What / the boys / watch on TV?
What are the boys watching on TV?
They're watching soccer.

1 What / the girl with the camera / wear?
2 What / the dog / do?
3 Where / the cat / sit?
4 How many people / stand up?
5 How many people / sit down?

16 **Complete the dialogue with the present progressive form of the verbs.**

Millie Hi, Kevin! Where are you? Are you at home?

Kevin Yes, I am. Why?

Millie What [1]_____ (you / do)?

Kevin I [2]_____ (watch) TV. What about you?

Millie Well, some of the kids from school are here.
We [3]_____ (have) a party!

Kevin A party? Oh yeah, I can hear music!

Millie That isn't music! That's Hayley!
She [4]_____ (try) to sing, but she [5]_____ (not sing), she [6]_____ (shout)!

Kevin Yeah, she's terrible! Are Ben and Harry there?

Millie Yes, they are, but they're boring!

Kevin Why? What [7]_____ (they / do)?

Millie They [8]_____ (play) games on the computer.

Kevin Cool! Who [9]_____ (win)?

Millie I have no idea! I [10]_____ (not watch) them! Come over and see!

Kevin OK. See you soon!

1 Sam's playing today

Check it out!

Go for it!   Good job!

1 🔘 Read and listen Who is the basketball team's star player?

a Zoe   b Teo   c Sam

Zoe Hi, I'm Zoe Ross. I'm writing an article about the basketball team for the school yearbook. Can I ask you some questions?

CC Yes, you can, but quickly! I'm watching the game.

Zoe Are we winning?

CC Yes, we are. Sam's playing today. He's our star player.

Zoe Who's Sam?

CC He's the tall boy with blond, wavy hair.

Zoe Oh, there's Teo! He's in my class. Is he playing well?

CC No, he isn't. He usually plays well, but he's playing badly today. Go for it, Sam!

Later …

Zoe Good job, Sam! You're a great player. How often do you practice?

Sam I practice every day. There's a big game in December.

Zoe Whose phone is ringing? Is it yours?

Sam Yes, it's mine. Oh, it's my mom!

Mom Sam, come home right now! You're in big trouble!

2 Comprehension Answer the questions.

Why is Zoe interviewing Coach Carson?
She is writing an article about basketball for the school yearbook.

1 Who is the basketball team's star player?
2 Who is in Zoe's class?
3 How often does Sam practice basketball?
4 Who calls Sam after the game?

Language focus

3 Dialogue focus Complete the dialogues with the questions in the box.

Can I ask you some questions   How often do you practice
Is he playing well   Who's Sam   Whose phone is ringing

1 **Zoe** I'm writing an article about the basketball team for the school yearbook. <u>Can I ask you some questions?</u>

CC Yes, you can, but quickly. I'm watching the game.

Zoe 1_____?

CC He's the tall boy with blond, wavy hair.

Zoe Oh, there's Teo! He's in my class.

2_____?

CC No, he isn't. He usually plays well, but he's playing badly today.

2 **Zoe** 3_____?

Sam I practice every day. There's a big game in December.

3 **Zoe** 4_____?

Is it yours?

Sam Yes, it's mine.

4 🔘 Listen and check. Then listen and repeat.

5 Focus on you Read the dialogue. Then write three similar dialogues. Use the verbs in the box.

do my homework   play basketball
play volleyball   study English
watch TV

every afternoon   every evening
on the weekend   on Wednesdays
three times a week

A What are you doing at the moment?   A How often do you play basketball?
B I'm playing basketball.   B I play basketball three times a week.

6 Pairwork Practice the dialogues in exercise 5.

Vocabulary

Physical descriptions

1 Match the descriptions with the people. Then listen and check.

1 _____   2 _____   3 _____   4 _____

a Maria is quite tall and quite slim. She has long, blond, curly hair, and she wears glasses.

b Ryan is short and slim. He has short, black, straight hair, a mustache, and a beard. His eyes are blue.

c Jake is very tall and very slim. He has short, red, spiky hair, and green eyes. He has freckles and he wears glasses.

d Emma is quite short and quite heavy. She has shoulder-length, brown, wavy hair, and brown eyes.

2 Complete the descriptions of these famous people. Then listen and check.

Look!

Adjective order
length + **color** + **style**
I have *long, blond, curly hair*.

Name Taylor Swift
Job singer / songwriter
Height 1.80 m
Weight 53 kg

Name Felipe Massa
Job Formula One driver
Height 1.65 m
Weight 58 kg

1 Taylor Swift is <u>tall</u> and ¹_____. She has ²_____, blond, ³_____ hair, and blue ⁴_____.

2 Felipe Massa is quite ¹_____ and ²_____. He has ³_____, black hair, and ⁴_____ eyes.

3 Pairwork Describe your favorite actor, singer, or sports personality to your partner.

A My favorite actor is Jack Black.
B What does he look like?
A He's quite short and heavy. He has brown eyes and short, wavy, brown hair. He has a mustache and a beard.

Simple present / Present progressive

Think!

● **Read the sentence. Then choose the correct alternative in the rules.**

Teo usually plays well, but he's playing badly today.
- We use the simple present to talk about [1]habits / actions in progress now.
- We use the present progressive to talk about [2]habits / actions in progress now.

Rules p.W2

1 Read the sentences. Underline the verbs.

I <u>listen</u> to the radio in the evening.
<u>Is</u> Cathy <u>doing</u> her homework now?
1 Do you study English every day?
2 She isn't listening to music at the moment.
3 He plays soccer once a week.
4 I'm writing an e-mail right now.
5 I always watch *Dancing with the Stars* on TV.
6 Tim doesn't play sports very often.

2 Look at the sentences in exercise 1. Circle the time expressions. Then complete the chart.

I listen to the radio (in the evening).
Is Cathy doing her homework (now)?

	Simple present	Present progressive
Time expressions	in the evening, …	now, …

3 Choose the correct answers.

She 's having / (has) dinner every day.
1 They 're listening / listen to a CD right now.
2 I 'm going / go to the movies every Saturday.
3 We aren't walking / don't walk to school in the mornings.
4 What do you do / are you doing at the moment?
5 How often does she play / is she playing volleyball?
6 Where's Lily? She's in the living room. She watches / 's watching TV.
7 Ms. Riley is the geography teacher. She doesn't teach / isn't teaching math.

4 Complete the sentences with the simple present or present progressive form of the verbs.

Rachel's a teacher. She <u>teaches</u> (teach) math at Richmond High School. At the moment, she <u>isn't teaching</u> (not teach) math. She's on vacation. She <u>'s sitting</u> (sit) in her yard and she <u>'s reading</u> (read) a book.

1 Simon and Clare are students. They [1]_____ (go) to Richmond High School. Right now, they [2]_____ (not study). It's Sunday and they [3]_____ (play) tennis.
2 My dad's a musician. He [1]_____ (play) in a band. Right now, he [2]_____ (not work). He [3]_____ (cook) dinner.
3 I'm a salesclerk. I [1]_____ (work) in New York City. Today is Sunday and I [2]_____ (not work). I [3]_____ (visit) a friend in Albany.

5 Game!

A **Read a time expression from the box.**

B **Make a correct sentence with the time expression.**

> at the moment   in the afternoon   never
> now   on the weekend   sometimes
> today   twice a week   usually

A never
B I never do homework on Saturdays.
(✓ = 1 point)
I'm never doing homework on Saturdays.
(✗ = 0 points)

Finished?

Write sentences with the time expressions from exercise 5.

We sometimes have a pizza on the weekend.

Making requests

1 **Listen and match the dialogues with the pictures. Listen again and repeat.**

1
A Can I open the window, please?
B Yes, you can. It's hot in here.
A Thank you.

2
A Can I borrow your English dictionary, Susana?
B Not now. I'm doing my homework. You can borrow it later.

3
A Can I have an ice cream, Mom?
B No, you can't! It's nearly dinner time.

1 _____
2 _____
3 _____

You ask	You answer
Can I open the window, please?	Yes, you can. / Yes, OK.
Can I borrow (*your dictionary*) please?	Not now. / You can (*borrow it*) later.
Can I (*have an ice cream*)?	No, you can't.

2 **Pronunciation** **Listen and repeat.**

Can I open the window, please?
Can I use your dictionary, please?
Can I have an ice cream?

Yes, you can.
Not now. I'm using it.
No, you can't.

3 **Listen and complete the requests. Check (✓) the positive replies and cross (✗) the negative replies.**

1 Can I _____? ☐
2 Can I _____? ☐
3 Can I _____? ☐

4 **Pairwork** **Make requests with the verbs in the box. Accept or reject your partner's requests.** 🎭

> borrow your book   close the window   copy your homework   have a snack
> sit next to you   use your cell phone   use your computer

Possessive pronouns

Possessive adjectives	Possessive pronouns
my	mine
your	yours
his	his
her	hers
its	–
our	ours
your	yours
their	theirs

Think!

Read the sentences. Are the rules true or false?

It's your phone. It's yours.

- ¹We use possessive adjectives before a noun.
- ²We use possessive pronouns before a noun.
- ³We use possessive pronouns to replace a possessive adjective and a noun.

Rules p.W3

1 **Complete the sentences with the correct possessive pronouns.**

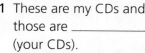

This isn't my cell phone. Where's _mine_ (my cell phone)?

1 These are my CDs and those are _____ (your CDs).

2 Martin's skateboard is blue. This isn't _____ (his skateboard).

3 "Whose pants are these? Are they Anna's?" "Yes, they're _____ (her pants)."

4 I don't like your classroom very much. I prefer _____ (our classroom).

5 That isn't their dog! _____ (Their dog) is big and brown.

6 These aren't our books. Are they _____ (your books)?

2 **Choose the correct answers.**

Here's (your) / yours ticket.

1 "Whose cap is this?" "It's **my / mine**."

2 Are these **theirs / their** jackets?

3 "Is this Lucy's cell phone?" "Yes, it's **her / hers**."

4 "Whose CDs are these?" "They're **our / ours**."

5 This is **your / yours** pen. **My / Mine** is blue.

Adverbs of manner
Regular adverbs

Adjective	Adverb
bad	bad**ly**
beautiful	beautiful**ly**
happy	happ**i**ly
fantastic	fantastic**ally**

Rules p.W3

Irregular adverbs

Adjective	Adverb
good	**well**
early	**early**
late	**late**
fast	**fast**

Rules p.W3

Think!

Read the sentences. Then choose the correct alternative in the rule.

He plays badly.

- Adverbs of manner come **before / after** the verb.

Rules p.W3

3 **Rewrite the sentences with adverbs.**

I have a quiet voice. I speak _quietly_.

1 My dad is a slow driver.
He drives _____.

2 You're a beautiful singer!
You sing _____.

3 Clara's a bad dancer.
Clara dances _____.

4 Fernando's a fast driver.
He drives _____.

5 Ana's a good swimmer.
She swims _____.

Finished?

Write true sentences about you or your family with the adverbs in the box.

| badly   fantastically   quietly |
| slowly   well |

My mom cooks well.

Basketball STARS coach young teens

Corey Monroe and Greg Griffin are gigantic men – Corey is 2.10 m tall and Greg is 2.12 m! They're basketball players and they play for a professional basketball team, the *Pittsburgh Players,* in Pennsylvania.

During the basketball season, Corey and Greg practice every morning and play in basketball games once or twice a week. But this week, they're doing something very different. They're coaching young teenagers on a summer basketball camp.

The *Pittsburgh Players Basketball Camp* is for boys and girls between the ages of twelve and fifteen. Some of the teenagers at the camp can already play basketball well, but others can't play at all. "That isn't a problem," Greg explains, "because there are different teams and different levels."

Laura Nolan, fourteen, is at the camp. "It's really cool!" she says, "Corey and Greg play basketball fantastically and they coach well. We're all in different basketball teams and I'm in a team with four of my friends from school! Every team has a name. Ours is *The Red Dragons*. We're playing in a championship and, right now, my team is doing well. I hope we win. The prize is a *Pittsburgh Players* basketball shirt with all the players' signatures!"

Reading

1 **Read the text. Correct the mistakes in the sentences below.**

Corey and Greg are quite short.
Corey and Greg are very tall.

1 Corey and Greg play for a professional volleyball team.
2 They usually practice once or twice a week.
3 This week they are playing in an important basketball game.
4 The *Pittsburgh Players Basketball Camp* is for young children.
5 The teenagers at the camp can play basketball well.
6 The name of Laura's team is the *Pittsburgh Players*.
7 Laura's friends aren't in her team.
8 Laura's team is playing badly in the championship at the moment.

Listening

2 🔘 **Bruno is at a summer camp. He's talking with his friend Christian on the phone. Listen to the conversation and choose the correct answers.**

Bruno is staying in … .
(a) Elkridge   **b** Baltimore

1 He's at a … .
  a sports camp   **b** theater camp

2 He … .
  a likes it   **b** doesn't like it

3 At the camp, he's doing … .
  a a dance course   **b** a drama course

4 He does the course … .
  a all day   **b** in the mornings

5 In the afternoons, … .
  a he plays soccer   **b** plays tennis

6 His favorite activity is … .
  a the drama course   **b** the parties

3 🔘 **Listen again. Complete Christian's questions.**

Where _are you?_

1 What type of _____ is it?
2 What's _____ like?
3 What _____ doing at the camp?
4 Do you _____ the course all day?
5 What other _____ are there?
6 _____ your favorite activity?

Speaking

4 **Pairwork** **Make a dialogue using the information below.** 🎭

A Your friend is attending one of the summer camps below. Call him / her. Ask him / her questions about the camp. Use exercise 3 to help you.

B You are attending one of the summer camps below. Student A calls you. Answer his / her questions.

At: Atlantic Theater Company
Courses in: drama, music, dance, and costume design
Afternoon activities: visits to The Statue of Liberty, The Rockerfeller Center, and The Theater Museum
Evening activities: movies, games, and quizzes. Plus a special visit to Broadway to see a musical!

Spotlight Performing Arts Camp
August 20th – 24th

S.P.I.K.E. Sports Camp
August 20th–24th
At: John Wood Teen Center
Courses in: tennis, soccer, volleyball, and basketball
Afternoon activities: swimming, art, cycling, and mini golf
Evening activities: movies, competitions, and parties!

Writing

5 **Use the information about your partner to complete this paragraph about what he / she is doing at the moment.**

At the moment, _____ is going to _____. The camp is at _____ and it's for _____ days. At the camp he / she is doing _____. In the afternoon he / she usually _____ and in the evening there are _____. His / Her favorite activity is _____. He / She thinks the camp is _____.

6 **Imagine you are attending one of the camps. Write a postcard to a friend with the information in exercise 4 and the information below.**

- name
- location
- type of camp
- activities
- favorite activity

2 Were you at the concert?

Check it out!

How come? It wasn't my fault.

1 🔘 **Read and listen Where was Sam last night?**

a at a game b at home c at a concert

Teo Were you at *The Ravens* concert last night?

Zoe Yes, I was. It was great! The atmosphere was electric. I love rock music!

Teo Yeah, so do I. It's cool!

Zoe So why weren't you at the concert?

Teo Because I was at basketball. There was a game yesterday.

Zoe Oh, yeah. So, what was the score?

Teo 96–32! We were terrible!

Zoe How come?

Teo Sam wasn't there. I don't understand it. He always comes to basketball practice.

Zoe There's Sam now. Let's ask him. Sam!

Sam arrives …

Sam Oh, hi, Zoe! Hello, Teo.

Teo Hello? Is that all you can say? Where were you last night?

Sam I was at home.

Teo At home? Why were you at home?

Sam It wasn't my fault. My parents were mad at me because my report card was bad. Now I can't play basketball.

Teo You can't play basketball? Oh no, that's a disaster for the team!

2 Comprehension Complete the sentences with adjectives from the dialogue.

The concert was _great_.

1 The atmosphere at the concert was _____.

2 The basketball team were _____.

3 Sam's parents were _____.

4 His report card was _____.

Language focus

3 Dialogue focus Write the sentences and questions in the correct order.

1 **Teo** Were you at *The Ravens* concert last night?

Zoe I / yes / was / great / it / was
<u>Yes, I was. It was great!</u>

The atmosphere was electric. I love rock music.

Teo do / yeah / I / so
1 _____.

It's cool!

2 **Teo** There was a game yesterday.

Zoe Oh, yeah.
so / score / the / what / was
2 _____?

Teo 96–32!
were / we / terrible
3 _____!

3 **Teo** where / you / last / were / night
4 _____?

Sam I was at home.

Teo At home?
were / why / at / you / home
5 _____?

Sam wasn't / it / fault /my
6 _____.

4 Listen and check. Then listen and repeat.

5 Focus on you Read the dialogue. Then write three similar dialogues with the expressions in the box.

> at a basketball game   at a concert   at a party
> at home   at the movies

A Where were you last night?
B I was <u>at home</u>.

6 Pairwork Practice your dialogues from exercise 5.

Vocabulary

Musical instruments and genres

1 🔘 **Listen to the musical instruments. Write the correct numbers next to the pictures.**

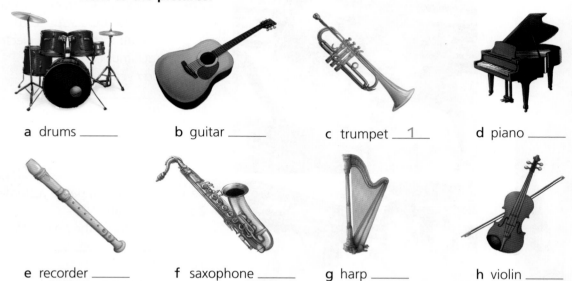

a drums _____

b guitar _____

c trumpet __1__

d piano _____

e recorder _____

f saxophone _____

g harp _____

h violin _____

Look!

To form the word for the person who plays a musical instrument we usually add **-ist** or **-er** to the musical instrument:

- guitar + **-ist** →
  guitarist
- violin + **-ist** →
  violinist
- harp + **-ist** →
  harpist
- trumpet + **-er** →
  trumpeter

2 🔘 **Listen and match the words in the box with the music you hear.**

classical   hip-hop   jazz   pop   reggae   rock

1 jazz

2 _____

3 _____

4 _____

5 _____

6 _____

3 Pairwork **Ask your partner about the kind of music he / she likes.** 🎭

A What's your favorite kind of music?

B I love rock. What about you?

A I love rock too. Do you like jazz?

B No, I don't. It's terrible! What about you?

A I like it.

🖱 **CD-ROM** ▶ **Workbook p. W10**

Grammar

be: Simple past
Affirmative and negative

	Affirmative	Negative
I	was	was not (wasn't)
you	were	were not (weren't)
he / she / it	was	was not (wasn't)
we / you / they	were	were not (weren't)

Think!

Complete the rules with the correct subject pronouns.

- You use *was* / *wasn't* with the subject pronouns [1]_____, [2]_____, [3]_____, and [4]_____.
- You use *were* / *weren't* with the subject pronouns [5]_____, [6]_____, and [7]_____.

Rules p.W8

1 Complete the sentences with *was* / *were* (✓) or *wasn't* / *weren't* (✗).

The boys _were_ at the basketball game. (✓)
1 The cars _____ in front of the house. (✗)
2 The party _____ cool. (✓)
3 The dogs _____ in the yard. (✓)
4 I _____ at the concert. (✗)
5 The movie _____ boring. (✓)
6 Eduardo _____ at school. (✗)
7 The guitarists _____ fantastic! (✓)
8 The singer _____ very good. (✗)

Past time expressions

yesterday morning / afternoon / evening
last night / Monday / week / month / year
a year / a week / two days / twenty minutes **ago**

Rules p.W8

2 Write the time expressions in the correct order.

~~an hour ago~~	last night	last week
~~last year~~	three months ago	two days ago
yesterday evening	yesterday morning	

1 _last year_
2 _____
3 _____
4 _____
5 _____
6 _____
7 _____
8 _an hour ago_

3 Look at the pictures. Complete the sentences with *was*, *were*, *wasn't*, or *weren't*, and a time expression.

1 Su-min _wasn't_ at the movies _last_ night.
2 Ivan _____ at school yesterday _____.
3 Emma and Stephanie _____ at home two hours _____.
4 Ryo _____ in Greece _____ summer.
5 Franco and Lola _____ at a party _____ Saturday.
6 Isabella _____ at the Grand Canyon a week _____.

Finished?

Guess where your partner was at these times. Write sentences. Then check with your partner.

last night at eight o'clock
last Saturday afternoon   one hour ago
this morning at seven o'clock
yesterday morning at nine o'clock

A You were at home last night at eight o'clock.
B No, I wasn't! I was at a basketball game.

CD-ROM Workbook pp. W10–W11

Communication

Agreeing and disagreeing

1 Read and listen. Check (✓) or cross (✗) the correct option. Listen and check. Then listen and repeat.

Katy Perry

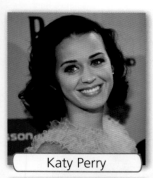

30 Seconds to Mars

	Emi	Luke
30 Seconds to Mars	✓	
Tokio Hotel		✗
Katy Perry		
Daniela Mercury		

Emi I like 30 Seconds to Mars.
Luke So do I. I think they're fantastic.
Emi And I like Tokio Hotel, too.
Luke Really? I don't.
Emi Look, it's Katy Perry. I don't like her.
Luke Neither do I.
Emi And I don't like Daniela Mercury.
Luke Really? I do. She's great.

Tokio Hotel

Daniela Mercury

You say	You answer
I like jazz.	So do I. / Really? I don't.
I don't like pop music.	Neither do I. / Really? I do.

2 **Pronunciation** Listen and repeat.

1 A I like pop music.
  B So do I.

2 A I like hip-hop.
  B Really? I don't.

3 A I don't like classical music.
  B Neither do I.

3 Listen and check (✓) or cross (✗) the correct box.

Jay-Z

Nelly Furtado

	Jay-Z	Nelly Furtado
Amy		
Scott		

4 **Pairwork** Give your opinions about the people below. Agree or disagree with your partner.

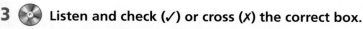

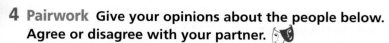
Beyoncé	Green Day	Kings of Leon	Linkin Park
	Madonna	Muse	Pink

be: Simple past
Interrogative and short answers

Interrogative	Short answers	
	Affirmative	Negative
Was I late?	Yes, I **was**.	No, I **wasn't**.
Were you late?	Yes, you **were**.	No, you **weren't**.
Was he / she / it late?	Yes, he / she / it **was**.	No, he / she / it **wasn't**.
Were we / you / they late?	Yes, we / you / they **were**.	No, we / you / they **weren't**.

Rules p.W9

1 **Write questions and answers.**

Michael Jackson / American? (✔)
Was Michael Jackson American?
Yes, he was.
1 Abel / at home / yesterday? (✘)
2 Jessica / in Brazil / last summer? (✔)
3 Jack and Ryan / at the soccer game / on Sunday (✔)
4 your cousins / at the party? (✘)
5 Johnny Depp / in the movie *Avatar*? (✘)

Question words + *was* / *were*

When	were you	*born?
Why	was he	at home?
Where	was she	on Sunday?
How old	were you	in 2004?

Rules p.W9

Look!

* We use the past tense of **be** to talk about birth.
When were you born? NOT ~~When are you born?~~

2 **Read the answers. Then write the questions.**

Where <u>were you last night</u>?
I was at the movies.
1 When _____? I was born in 1996.
2 When _____? I was in Spain last summer.
3 How _____? The concert was fantastic!
4 Where _____? John Lennon was born in Liverpool.
5 Why _____? His parents were mad because his school report was bad.
6 How old _____ in June? I was thirteen.

3 **Read the factfile. Then complete the dialogue.**

Name	Jimi Hendrix
Profession	Rock guitarist
Nationality	American
Date of birth	November 27th, 1942

A Who was Jimi Hendrix?
B He ¹_____ a rock guitarist.
A What nationality ²_____?
B He was American.
A When ³_____?
B He was born on ⁴_____.

4 **Game!** **Ask and answer questions about the famous people below.**

Name	Ella Fitzgerald
Profession	Jazz singer
Nationality	American
Date of birth	April 25th, 1917

Name	Amadeus Mozart
Profession	Classical music composer
Nationality	Austrian
Date of birth	January 27th, 1756

Finished?

Write quiz questions with be about three other famous musicians or singers from the past. Ask the class your questions.

Who was Elvis Presley?
What nationality was he?

Bono – a living legend

Bono is a very famous Irish singer. He is the lead singer of the rock band U2. His real name isn't Bono. It's Paul David Hewson. Bono is his nickname. It's an abbreviation of *Bona Vox*. That means "good voice" in Latin.

Bono was born on May 10th, 1960, in Dublin, Ireland. When he was a teenager, he was a student at Mount Temple Comprehensive School. The other members of the band – the drummer Larry Mullen and the guitarists David Evans (The Edge) and Adam Clayton – were students there, too. At first the name of their band was Feedback, then The Hype, and finally U2.

Bono writes the lyrics for U2's songs. They often have social and political themes. The band's first international hit song was in 1980. Its title was "I Will Follow" and it was popular in Ireland, the U.K. and the U.S. By the mid-1980s, U2 was famous all over the world and Bono was a superstar.

In 1985, Bono and U2 were part of a special project to help poor people in Africa and they were performers at a famous charity concert called Live Aid. Today, Bono does a lot of work to help poor people around the world and is a supporter of the human rights organization, Amnesty International.

Live Aid, London, 1985

Reading

1 Read the text. Are the sentences true or false? Correct the false sentences.

Bono is a British singer. *False. Bono is an Irish singer.*

1 He's a member of the rock band U2.
2 He was born in 1962.
3 The members of U2 were at the same school.
4 The first name of the band was The Hype.
5 The band's first international hit song was in 1984.
6 Bono wasn't at the Live Aid concert.
7 Today, Bono does a lot of charity work.

Listening

2 🔘 **Listen and choose the correct answers.**

1 Elvis Presley was … .
   a a pop singer   ⓑ a rock 'n' roll singer   c a rock singer

2 His nickname was … .
   a The King   b The Star   c The Rock

3 He was born in … .
   a 1935   b 1958   c 1965

4 He was born in the state of … .
   a Massachusetts   b Mississippi   c Minnesota

5 When he was a teenager his favorite kinds of music were … .
   a classical and jazz   b pop, rock, and rap   c gospel, blues, and country

6 Elvis was also … .
   a an athlete   b a drummer   c an actor

Speaking

3 **Ask and answer questions about Shakira and Justin Timberlake.**

- What / full name?
  A What is Shakira's full name?
  B Shakira Isabel Mebarak Ripoll
- Why / famous?
- Where / born?

- When / born?
  A When was she born?
  B She was born on February 2nd, 1977.
- When / first international hit?
- What / international hit in (2002 / 2006 …)?

Name	Shakira
Full name	Shakira Isabel Mebarak Ripoll
Date of birth	February 2nd, 1977
Place of birth	Baranquilla, Colombia
Job	Pop singer and songwriter
International hits	2002: *Whenever, Wherever*
	2006: *Hips Don't Lie*
	2009: *She Wolf*

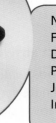

Name	Justin Timberlake
Full name	Justin Randall Timberlake
Date of birth	January 31st, 1981
Place of birth	Memphis, U.S.
Job	Pop singer, actor, and songwriter
International hits	2002: *Cry Me a River*, *Rock Your Body*
	2006: *My love*

Writing

4 **Complete the paragraph about Shakira. Use the information from exercise 3.**

Shakira is a Colombian pop singer and <u>songwriter</u>. She ¹_____ born on
²_____ in Baranquilla, ³_____. Her first international hit was in
⁴_____. It ⁵_____ a song called *Whenever, Wherever*. Her other hits
include ⁶_____ and *She Wolf*.

5 **Write a paragraph about Justin Timberlake. Use the information from exercise 3. Then write a paragraph about your favorite pop singer.**

Vocabulary

1 Copy and complete the chart. Match the words to the categories. Some words can go in two categories.

> beard   black   blond   blue
> brown   curly   freckles   glasses
> green   heavy   long   mustache
> red   ~~short~~   shoulder-length   spiky
> ~~straight~~   tall   thin   wavy

body	eyes	face	hair
short			short straight

2 Complete each sentence with an appropriate word.

My mom has long, _blond_ hair.

1 Ellen has red hair and _____ on her face.
2 Eduardo has a mustache, but he doesn't have a _____.
3 Yumi wears _____.
4 Lucas has big, blue _____.
5 Al is tall, but he isn't slim. He's quite _____.

3 Find five more kinds of music and five more musical instruments in the word square.

R	E	C	O	R	D	E	R
G	Q	L	T	H	R	P	E
U	G	A	Z	I	U	J	G
I	O	S	L	P	M	A	G
T	H	S	X	H	S	Z	A
A	P	I	J	O	L	Z	E
R	O	C	K	P	H	M	A
S	P	A	P	I	A	N	O
V	I	L	K	S	R	R	E
A	T	R	U	M	P	E	T

Kinds of music   Instruments
reggae   _recorder_

1 _____   6 _____
2 _____   7 _____
3 _____   8 _____
4 _____   9 _____
5 _____   10 _____

Grammar

4 Complete the dialogues with the simple present or the present progressive form of the verbs.

A Where's Jun? Is _he doing_ (he / do) his homework?
B No, _he isn't_. He 's _watching_ (watch) TV.

1 A What time _____ (Lally / get up) on the weekend?
  B She always _____ (get up) late. She never _____ (go) to bed before 11 p.m!

2 A _____ (Nathan / use) the computer at the moment?
  B Yes, he _____. He _____ (write) an e-mail.

3 A _____ (Tomas / play) tennis well today?
  B No, he _____. He usually _____ (play) well, but he _____ (play) badly today.

5 Complete the sentences with the correct possessive pronouns.

This book's _yours_! It has your name on it!

1 "Here's your MP3 player." "It isn't _____. I don't have an MP3 player."
2 "Is this Maria's journal?" "Yes, it's _____."
3 "These aren't our CDs! Where are _____?"
4 "Is this the boys' ball?" "No, it isn't. _____ is black and blue."
5 "Whose phone is this?" "Ask that boy. I think it's _____."

6 Choose the correct answers.

Carolina is a (good) / well actor.

1 My dad speaks English very **bad / badly**.
2 Can you speak **slow / slowly**, please?
3 Be **quiet / quietly**, please!
4 A horse can run **fast / fastly**.
5 Flavio is a very **happily / happy** baby.

7 Complete the text with the adverb forms of the adjectives.

Tom and Amy are cousins, but they're very different. Tom always goes to school _early_ (early) but Amy often arrives [1]_____ (late). Tom studies [2]_____ (happy) and does his school work [3]_____ (quick) and [4]_____ (good). Amy works [5]_____ (quiet), but very [6]_____ (slow).

8 Rewrite the sentences in the simple past.

Tim is at basketball practice now.
~~Tim was at basketball practice~~ yesterday.

1 The students aren't in their classroom.
This morning _____.

2 Nikki's hair isn't short.
Last year, _____.

3 Matt and Ellen are in the living room.
_____ ten minutes ago.

4 Is Fergie your favorite singer?
_____ when you were ten?

5 Are your teachers friendly?
_____ at elementary school?

9 Complete the dialogues with the simple past form of the verb _be_.

1 A Why <u>was</u> he famous?
B He ¹_____ a fantastic opera singer.
A ²_____ he American?
B No, he ³_____. He ⁴_____ from Italy.
A When ⁵_____ he born?
B He ⁶_____ born in the 1930s.

Pavarotti

2 A Who ¹_____ she?
B She ²_____ a famous singer.
A What nationality ³_____ she?
B She ⁴_____ South African.
A What ⁵_____ her nickname?
B It ⁶_____ Mama Afrika.

Miriam Makeba

3 A Who ¹_____ they?
B They ²_____ a famous pop group.
A ³_____ they British?
B No, they ⁴_____. They ⁵_____ from Sweden.
A What ⁶_____ their first hit?
B It was a song called _Waterloo_.

ABBA

Got it?

10 Complete the message with the simple present, present progressive, or simple past form of the verbs.

○ ○ ○   ✉   ▭

Hi, Laura

I'm sorry I (wasn't) (not be) at your party last Friday. We ¹_____ (be) at my grandma's house. It ²_____ (be) her 80ᵗʰ birthday party! It ³_____ (be) a good evening.

It's very hot here today, and I ⁴_____ (sit) in the yard. I ⁵_____ (do) my vacation homework and I ⁶_____ (listen) to Lady Gaga on my MP3 player. I think she sings beautifully. I always ⁷_____ (listen) to music when I ⁸_____ (study)! What ⁹_____ (you / do) right now? Are you on vacation?

Yesterday, Mom and I ¹⁰_____ (be) at the Kenwood Plaza. It's an enormous shopping mall and we ¹¹_____ (go) there two or three times a year. We usually ¹²_____ (shop) there at Christmas and before the school year ¹³_____ (start) in September. It's really cool! Dad ¹⁴_____ (call) me! He ¹⁵_____ (want) to check my homework!

Bye for now. Write soon!

Nikki x

11 Answer the questions.

1 Where was Nikki last Friday?
_____

2 What is she doing at the moment?
_____

3 Where were Nikki and her mom yesterday?
_____

4 How often do they go there?
_____

5 Why is Nikki's dad calling her?
_____

A history of popular music

Rock 'n' roll was born in the U.S. in the 1950s. It was a mix of blues and country music. Elvis Presley was the first rock 'n' roll superstar. Soon rock 'n' roll was popular in other countries. A British band, The Beatles, was world famous in the 1960s. Their music was very influential on modern pop and rock.

In the 1970s, rock music, with bands like Pink Floyd and Led Zeppelin, was very popular. For some people these groups were too serious, and so glam rock (short for "glamorous") was born. David Bowie and Elton John were its leaders. Elton John was famous for his incredible clothes and crazy glasses. In 1976, punk rock, a type of rebellious rock music, was born in the U.K. and the U.S. The Sex Pistols, The Clash, and The Ramones were important punk bands. The 1980s was the period of stadium rock. Its superstars were Bruce Springsteen, Queen, and U2. Their concerts were in enormous stadiums. In 1981 there were 130,000 people at the Queen concert in the Maracanã Stadium in Rio de Janeiro! Hip-hop is a popular music style today. Beyoncé and Jay-Z are popular hip-hop superstars.

1 Answer the questions.

1 Where and when was rock 'n' roll born?
2 What nationality were The Beatles?
3 Who were the leaders of the glam rock era?
4 When was punk rock born?
5 Who were the stadium rock superstars of the 1980s?
6 How many people were at the Queen concert in Rio de Janeiro in 1981?

2 Find and circle all the kinds of music in the text.

3 Focus on you Find out about two singers or bands who were important in the history of popular music in your country. Prepare a short presentation about them.
You can use the questions to help you.

- Where were they born?
- When were they born?
- What kind of music were / are they famous for?
- What are their famous songs?

Speaking and writing

1 I can describe a person's physical appearance.
                                                    A2

Charlie is tall and slim.

1 _____
2 _____
3 _____
4 _____
5 _____

Got it? ____ / 5

2 I can write about when I do things.   **A2**

I go to the movies every week.

1 _____
2 _____
3 _____
4 _____
5 _____

Got it? ____ / 5

3 I can make requests.   **A2**

Can I open the window?

1 _____
2 _____
3 _____
4 _____
5 _____

Got it? ____ / 5

4 I ask and answer questions about what music I like.   **A2**

Do you like jazz?

1 _____
2 _____
3 _____
4 _____
5 _____

Got it? ____ / 5

5 I can ask and answer questions about famous musicians.   **A2**

Who was Elvis Presely?

1 _____
2 _____
3 _____
4 _____
5 _____

Got it? ____ / 5

6 I can agree and disagree.   **A2**

Really? I don't like her.

1 _____
2 _____
3 _____
4 _____
5 _____

Got it? ____ / 5

Reading, listening, and writing

		Got It?		
		Yes	I'm not sure	No
7 I can understand a text about a famous singer.	A2	☐	☐	☐
8 I can identify musical instruments and different types of music.	A2	☐	☐	☐
9 I can write about what I did yesterday.	A2	☐	☐	☐
10 I can write a postcard.	A2	☐	☐	☐

3 You failed another test!

1 💿 **Read and listen** **What does Sam want to be?**

> **a** a doctor **b** a lawyer **c** a basketball player

Teo   I don't believe it, Sam. You failed another math test. Why aren't you studying?

Sam   I don't want to be a doctor or a lawyer. I want to be a basketball player.

Teo   But Sam, we can't win without you.

Sam   Look at Michael Jordan. He wasn't great at school, but he played for the *Chicago Bulls* and he won eight NBA championships.

Teo   Michael Jordan! Are you serious? Do you think you're Michael Jordan? Get real!

CC   Sam, I want to talk with you in my office.

In Coach Carson's office …

Sam   Yes, Coach.

CC   I spoke to your mom yesterday.

Sam   Really? That's great. Can I play again now?

CC   I'm sorry, but you can't. You did badly at school again and I agree with your mom.

Sam   What? But Coach …

CC   Don't make excuses, Sam. The math test on Wednesday is your last chance. You're off the team for now.

2 Comprehension **Complete the sentences with Sam (S), Michael Jordan (MJ), or Coach Carson (CC).**

    <u>S</u> failed another test.

1 _____ won eight NBA championships.

2 _____ spoke with Sam's mom.

3 _____ agrees with Sam's mom.

4 _____ is off the team for now.

Check it out!

I don't believe it	Get real!
Are you serious?	last chance

Language focus

3 Dialogue focus Find and correct the mistakes in the dialogues.

1 – You failed another math test.

1

Teo I don't believe it, Sam. You failed another (history) test. Why aren't you studying?

Sam I don't want to be an engineer or a lawyer. I want to be a soccer player.

2

Sam Look at Michael Jordan. He wasn't great at school, but he played for the *Boston Celtics* and he won twelve NBA championships.

Teo Michael Jordan! Are you serious? Do you think you're Michael Jordan? Get real!

3

CC I spoke to your dad yesterday.

Sam Really? That's great. Can I play again now?

CC I'm sorry, but you can't. You did badly in your last game.

4 🔘 Listen and check. Then listen and repeat.

5 Focus on you Use the information below to write about the sports personalities.

Name Michael Jordan
Sport Basketball player
Team Chicago Bulls
NBA Championships 8

Name Ayrton Senna
Sport Formula 1 racing driver
Team Toleman, Lotus, McClaren, and Williams
Formula 1 World Championships 3

My favorite sports star is Michael Jordan. He played for the "Chicago Bulls". He won eight NBA championships.

Name Pelé
Sport Soccer player
Team Santos and Brazil
World Cups 6

Name Jackie Joyner-Kersee
Sport Athlete
Team U.S. Olympic team
Gold medals 3

6 Pairwork Choose a sports personality from the sports cards in exercise 5. Then tell your partner about him / her. 🎭

thirty-one

Vocabulary

Jobs

1  **Match the pictures with the jobs in the box. Then listen and check.**

| accountant | doctor | electrician | engineer | factory worker | hairdresser |
| ~~journalist~~ | lawyer | office worker | postal worker | salesclerk | teacher |

journalist _____ _____ _____

_____ _____ _____ _____

_____ _____ _____ _____

Look!

The most common ending for jobs is **-er**. Other common endings are **-ist**, **-ian**, **-man**, **-ant**, and **-or**.

2 Write an example for each ending. Choose from the jobs in exercise 1.

-er *teacher*   -ant ³_____

-ist ¹_____   -or ⁴_____

-ian ²_____

3 Write the name of the job.

1 I sell things in a store. s a l e s c l e r k
2 I write articles for a newspaper. j _ _ _ _ _ _ _ _ _
3 I work in a salon. I cut and style people's hair. h _ _ _ d _ _ _ _ _ _
4 I deliver letters and parcels. p _ _ _ _ _ w _ _ _ _ _
5 I design machines and engines. e _ _ _ _ _ _ _
6 I work in a factory. We make cars. f _ _ _ _ _ _ w _ _ _ _ _

4 Pairwork **Tell your partner what job you want to do when you leave school.**

A What do you want to be?
B I want to be a …

CD-ROM **Workbook p.W16**

Simple past: Regular verbs
Affirmative

I / you / he / she / it / we / you / they	play**ed**

> **Think!**
>
> ● **Read the sentences. Then check (✓) the correct ending for the rule.**
>
> We wat**ched** the soccer game last week.
> I tal**ked** with Victoria yesterday.
>
> ● We use the simple past to talk about events and situations …
> **a** that started in the past. ☐
> **b** that started and finished in the past. ☑
>
> **Rules p.W14**

1 Complete the sentences with the simple past form of the verbs in the box.

> ask   help   listen   open   start
> talk   wait   ~~walk~~   wash

I **walked** to school yesterday.
1 We _____ to the new Skank CD.
2 My dad _____ me with my homework.
3 The movie _____ at eight o'clock.
4 He _____ for my name and my address.
5 He _____ his hair in the shower.
6 I _____ at the bus stop for 30 minutes.
7 I _____ the window because it was hot.
8 She _____ on the phone for two hours.

Simple past: Regular verbs
Spelling variations

Most verbs: + -ed		
play	→	play**ed**
Verbs ending in -e: + -d		
live	→	live**d**
use	→	use**d**
Verbs ending in -y: -y + -ied		
study	→	stud**ied**
cry	→	cr**ied**
Verbs ending in vowel + consonant: double consonant + -ed		
stop	→	stop**ped**
prefer	→	prefer**red**
Rules p.W14		

2 Read about what Lucy and Daniel did yesterday. Complete the sentences with the simple past form of the verbs in the box.

> arrive   call   help   stop   study
> talk   ~~wait~~

① Yesterday morning, I had a terrible bus journey to Atlanta! I **waited** for 40 minutes because the bus was late. Then the bus ¹_____ every three or four minutes for passengers. I finally ²_____ in Atlanta at lunchtime!

Yesterday morning, I ¹_____ science and then I ²_____ my mom with the household chores. In the afternoon, I ³_____ my friend, Carly, and we ⁴_____ for an hour. ②

3 ◉ Pronunciation Listen and repeat.

/d/	/t/	/ɪd/
listen**ed**	ask**ed**	want**ed**

Rules p.W14

4 ◉ Listen and write the verbs in the correct column.

> ~~decided~~   ended   ~~helped~~   ~~lived~~
> needed   opened   started
> talked   watched

/d/	/t/	/ɪd/
lived	_helped_	_decided_
1_____	2_____	4_____
	3_____	5_____
		6_____

> **Finished?**

Write about what you did yesterday evening and last Saturday. Use the verbs on this page.

Yesterday evening, I watched TV, and I talked with my mom.

Apologizing and making excuses

1 🔘 **Listen to the dialogues and choose the correct answers. Listen and check. Then listen and repeat.**

1

David	Excuse me, Mr. Clarke.
Mr. Clarke	Yes, David. What is it?
David	I'm sorry, but I don't have my ¹homework / English book.
Mr. Clarke	Where is it?
David	I left it ²at home / on the bus.
Mr. Clarke	Never mind. ³**Bring it tomorrow / Work with Naomi.**
David	Thanks, Mr. Clarke.

2

Pam	Hi, Sal. Do you have my Red Hot Chili Peppers ¹CD / DVD?
Sal	Oh, I'm sorry. It's at ²school / home.
Pam	It doesn't matter. Give it to me on ³Saturday / Monday.

You say	You answer
I'm sorry.	Never mind.
	Don't worry.
	It doesn't matter.

2 🔘 **Pronunciation** /ɑ/ **and** /oʊ/. **Listen and repeat.**

        /ɑ/   /oʊ/

Your Red Hot Chili Peppers CD is at home.

3 🔘 **Listen and write the words in the correct row** /ɑ/ **or** /oʊ/.

don't   go   got   ~~home~~   ~~hot~~   on   photo   sorry   stop   woke

| /ɑ/ | hot | 1_____ | 2_____ | 3_____ | 4_____ |
| /oʊ/ | home | 5_____ | 6_____ | 7_____ | 8_____ |

Look!

Use *Excuse me* to attract attention and *Sorry* to apologize.
- *Excuse me*. What time is it?
- *I'm sorry*, I forgot your birthday.

4 🔘 **Listen to the conversations. Choose the correct answers.**

1 Beth can't play tennis because … .
  a she has a swimming lesson
  b she has a piano lesson
  c she has an English lesson

2 Alex left his jacket … .
  a at school
  b on the bus
  c at the bus station

3 Toby doesn't have his … .
  a history book
  b science book
  c geography book

4 Emma is late for class because … .
  a she woke up late
  b the bus was late
  c the train was late

5 **Pairwork** **Apologize for the actions in the box. Answer your partner with a suitable reply.** 🎭

you ate your friend's chocolate   you can't play volleyball
you forgot your friend's party   you left your friend's CD on the bus
you read your friend's journal   you wrote on your friend's notebook

Grammar

Simple past: Irregular verbs

Base form	Simple past
come	came
do	did
drink	drank
eat	ate
get	got
give	gave
go	went
have	had
leave	left
make	made
read	read
ride	rode
run	ran
see	saw
speak	spoke
spend	spent
take	took
travel	traveled
win	won
write	wrote

Rules p.W15

1 Complete the sentences with the simple past form of the verbs.

Helen _came_ to my birthday party last year.
1 I _____ (write) three e-mails last night.
2 We _____ (read) *The Hobbit* last year.
3 They _____ (take) the bus to the mall.
4 I _____ (see) Matt last week.
5 Mom _____ (make) pizza yesterday.
6 They _____ (go) to Greece on vacation.

2 Complete the message with the simple past form of the verbs.

Hi, Jonathan!
Thanks for your postcard from Miami! Last summer, my family _went_ (go) on vacation to Florianópolis. We
¹_____ (have) a great time! We ²_____ (try)
windsurfing and I ³_____ (go) diving! Then we
⁴_____ (take) a bus around the island and I
⁵_____ (see) some cool places! I ⁶_____ (meet)
two American girls on the bus and I ⁷_____ (speak)
English all day! The food ⁸_____ (be) fantastic and I
⁹_____ (eat) some amazing fish!

Write soon!

Gabriel

3 Complete the text with simple past form of the verbs.

Rubens Barrichello _was born_
(be born) in São Paulo in 1972.
His family ¹_____ (love)
racing. His uncle ²_____
(have) an American Formula 3
racing team and some of his
cousins ³_____ (ride) karts.
When he was six years old, his
grandfather ⁴_____ (give)
him a kart. He ⁵_____ (start)
racing when he was nine and he
⁶_____ (come) third in his first
official race. Two years later, he ⁷_____
(become) the Brazilian Junior Karting Champion.
In 1990, he ⁸_____ (leave) Brazil and
⁹_____ (travel) to Europe. In 1993, he joined
the Jordan Formula 1 racing team and between
1993 and 2005 he competed for Jordan,
Stewart, Ferrari, and Honda. Today, he races
for Williams-Cosworth. Barrichello ¹⁰_____
(win) his first Grand Prix race in Germany in 2000
and he is now a successful and world famous
Formula 1 driver.

4 Game! Make a story.

go	travel	stay	visit	meet
speak	see	eat	drink	spend

Work in groups of three.

A **Make a simple past sentence with the first verb in the list.**

B **Repeat the sentence and add a sentence with the simple past form of the second verb.**

C **Repeat the sentences and add another sentence**

Tell the class your story!

A Last year, I went to Australia.
B Last year, I went to Australia. I traveled by airplane, car, and train.
C Last year, I ...

Finished?

Write the story you invented in exercise 4.

CD-ROM Workbook pp. W16–17

thirty-five
35

Christopher Columbus

Christopher Columbus was born in Genoa, Italy, in 1451. He was a sailor and an explorer, and his ambition was to travel west to Asia. In the 15th century Asia was important for commerce and a lot of sailors went there. They always sailed east and their journey was long and dangerous. Columbus believed that the world was round and that the short route to Asia was west.

In 1492 King Ferdinand and Queen Isabella of Spain gave Columbus money for his journey. Three ships, the *Niña*, the *Pinta*, and the *Santa Maria*, left Spain on August 3rd, 1492. The journey was very long, but after two months, they arrived on an island in the Caribbean. Columbus and his sailors called the island San Salvador (Holy Savior). Columbus thought he was in India and that the people on the island were Indians. He returned to Spain a hero and he brought gold, animals, and new plants to Europe.

Columbus's journey was important because he discovered the New World – the world of the Americas. Today, the U.S. has a holiday on October 12th to celebrate Christopher Columbus's first journey to the New World. It's called *Columbus Day*.

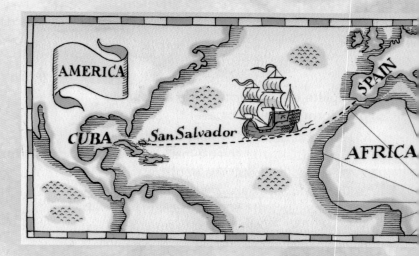

Reading

1 **Read the text. Then complete the summary about Christopher Columbus.**

Christopher Columbus was born in Genoa, <u>Italy</u> in 1451. He believed that the world was ¹_____ and that it was possible to sail ²_____ from Europe to Asia. In 1492 ³_____ and Queen Isabella of Spain gave him money for his journey. Columbus and his sailors traveled from Spain in ⁴_____ ships. They arrived on an island two ⁵_____ later. Columbus thought he was in ⁶_____ but he was in the ⁷_____. He returned to ⁸_____ a hero and he brought gold and new ⁹_____ to Europe. Today in the U.S., people celebrate his life on ¹⁰_____ 12th – *Columbus Day*.

Listening

2 🔘 **Listen to the information about George Washington. Choose the correct answers.**

George Washington was born in (1732)/ 1832.

1 At the time, America was a **French / British** colony.
2 He joined the army when he was **22 / 20** years old.
3 George fought for Britain in a war against **French and Indian people / American colonists**.
4 American colonists declared their independence from Britain in **1776 / 1789**.
5 In the War of Independence, Washington was the Commander of the **American army / British army**.
6 He became the **first / second** President of the U.S.
7 He was President for **five / eight** years.

Speaking

3 **Choose one of the famous people below. Then use the notes to make an oral presentation of their lives.**

William Shakespeare	
1564	was born in Stratford-upon-Avon, England
1582	marries Anne Hathaway and has three children
1592	moves to London, becomes an actor and a successful writer
1596–1606	writes many famous plays including *Romeo and Juliet*, *Hamlet*, and *The Merchant of Venice*
1599	opens his famous theater, *The Globe*
1610	returns to Stratford-upon-Avon
1616	dies

Marie Curie	
1867	was born in Warsaw, Poland
1891	goes to the Sorbonne University in Paris; studies physics, chemistry, and math
1895	marries the physicist Pierre Curie
1897	works as a teacher and continues her research
1902	discovers the radioactive elements *polonium* and *radium* with her husband
1906	husband dies; becomes a professor at the Sorbonne
1911	wins the Nobel Prize for Chemistry
1934	dies

be or not to be,
t is the Ques—
: whether 'tis

88
Ra

84
Po

Writing

4 **Write a short paragraph about the life of one of the people in exercise 3.**

1 💿 **Read and listen** **What are Zoe and Sam talking about?**

> **a** school   **b** sports   **c** movies

Sam What did you do last night?

Zoe I watched *Spider-Man 3* on TV. Did you watch it?

Sam No, I didn't. I didn't watch TV last night. But I saw it at the movies ages ago! I didn't like it. It was awful! Did you like it?

Zoe Yes, I did. I love Tobey Maguire! He's my favorite actor!

Sam Did you like the movie, or did you like Tobey Maguire?

Zoe I liked them both! What kind of movies do you like?

Sam I like action and science fiction movies. My favorite movies are *Sherlock Holmes* and *Star Trek*. I bet you like love stories!

Zoe Yes, but I like fantasy movies, too. I got the DVD of *Alice in Wonderland* for my birthday. Do you want to come and watch it with me?

Sam OK! Oh, no, I can't! I have a math test on Wednesday!

Zoe Oh, come on, Sam! Get a life!

Sam You're right! Let's watch the movie! I can study tomorrow …

2 Comprehension **Answer the questions.**

What movie was on TV last night? *Spider-Man 3*

1 Who is Zoe's favorite actor?

2 What are Sam's favorite movies?

3 What do Zoe and Sam decide to do?

Check it out!

It was awful!	Get a life!
I bet …	You're right!

Language focus

3 Dialogue focus Write the dialogues in the correct order.

1
- I watched *Spider-Man 3* on TV. Did you watch it?
- What did you do last night?
- No, I didn't. I didn't watch TV last night.

Sam   *What did you do last night?*
Zoe   _____
Sam   _____

2
- Yes, I did. I love Tobey Maguire! He's my favorite actor!
- I liked them both!
- I saw it at the movies ages ago! I didn't like it. It was awful! Did you like it?
- Did you like the movie, or did you like Tobey Maguire?

Sam   _____
Zoe   _____
Sam   _____
Zoe   _____

3
- Yes, but I like fantasy movies, too.
- What kind of movies do you like?
- I like action and science fiction movies. My favorite movies are *Sherlock Holmes* and *Star Trek*. I bet you like love stories!

Zoe   _____
Sam   _____
Zoe   _____

4 🔘 **Listen and check. Then listen and repeat.**

5 Focus on you Read the dialogue. Then write three similar dialogues with activities in the box.

> do homework   ~~go for a pizza~~   play computer games
> watch TV   read a book   surf the Internet

A What did you do last night?
B *I went for a pizza.*

6 Pairwork Practice your dialogues from exercise 5.

Vocabulary

Movies

1 **Match the pictures with the kinds of movies.**

> action movie   animated movie   comedy   fantasy movie
> horror movie   love story   science fiction movie   thriller

1 _____

2 _____

3 _____

4 _____

5 _____

6 _____

Look!

a **comedy**
a **thriller**
a **love story**
but:
an **action movie**
an **animated movie**
a **fantasy movie**
a **horror movie**
a **science fiction movie**

7 _____

8 _____

2 💿 **Listen and check. Then listen and repeat.**

3 💿 **Listen to the movie extracts. What kind of movies do they come from?**

1 _a love story_   3 _____   5 _____

2 _____   4 _____   6 _____

4 **Pairwork** **Tell your partner about your favorite kinds of movies.** 🎭

A What is your favorite kind of movie?
B I really like animated movies. My favorite movie is "*Ponyo*".
   What about you?
A I like animated movies, too but I prefer action movies.
   My favorite movie is "*X-Men Origins: Wolverine*".

Grammar

Simple past
Negative

I / you /		answer
he / she / it /	did not / didn't	go
we / you / they		come

> ### Think!
>
> - **Write the simple past negative form of these verbs.**
>
> | play | played | ¹_____ |
> |---|---|---|
> | drink | drank | ²_____ |
> | win | won | ³_____ |
>
> **Read the rule. Choose the correct alternative.**
>
> - We form the simple past negative of regular and irregular verbs ⁴**in the same way / in different ways**.
>
> **Rules p.W20**

1 **Rewrite the sentences with the simple past negative form.**

I saw the movie on TV.
I didn't see the movie on TV.
1 You sang that song very well.
2 Jake went to school yesterday.
3 Mari wore her new jeans to the party.
4 Ana and Luis played tennis on Monday.
5 I liked *Avatar* very much.
6 We bought popcorn at the movie theater.

2 **Rewrite the sentences with true information.**

Kung-Fu Panda won the Oscar for the best animated movie in 2009. (*Wall-E*)
"Kung Fu Panda" didn't win the Oscar for the best animated movie in 2009. "Wall-E" won it.
1 Alfred Hitchcock directed love stories. (thrillers)
_____
_____
2 Ben Stiller starred in *Star Wars*. (*Night at the Museum*)
_____
_____
3 Corbin Bleu played the part of Troy in *High School Musical*. (Zac Efron)
_____
_____

4 Madonna sang in the musical *Hairspray*. (John Travolta)
_____
_____
5 Disney made the animated movie *Monsters vs. Aliens*. (Dreamworks)
_____
_____
6 Mike Myers was the voice of Donkey in *Shrek*. (Eddie Murphy)
_____
_____

3 **Complete the message with the simple past affirmative or negative form of the verbs.**

Hi, Rob

I'm sorry I <u>didn't meet</u> (not meet) you at the movie theater yesterday. I was really late and when I ¹_____ (arrive), you weren't there. I ²_____ (try) to call you but my cell phone ³_____ (not have) any credit!

I'm really sorry! It was a bad day…

In the morning, I ⁴_____ (not go) to my tennis lesson, I ⁵_____ (get up) late! Then, in the afternoon, I ⁶_____ (go) to the shopping mall because I ⁷_____ (want) to buy Jay-Z's new CD. I ⁸_____ (not take) my jacket because it was hot, but my money was in the jacket! I was really angry! And, of course, I ⁹_____ (not buy) the CD!

Then, in the evening … well, you know about the evening …

I'm sorry! Are you mad at me?

Ellie

> ### Finished?

Check (✓) the things you did yesterday and cross (✗) the things you didn't do. Then write a sentence about each thing.

1 get up early	☒	3 go shopping	☐
I didn't get up early.		4 meet friends	☐
2 play sports	☐	5 watch a movie	☐

Buying a movie ticket

1 🔘 **Listen and read the dialogue. Write the missing numbers from the box. Listen and check. Then listen and repeat.**

> 1 2 5 7 8 25 30

A What time is the next showing of *Up*, please?
B It's at ⅛ p.m.
A OK. Can I have ¹___ adult ticket and ²___ children's tickets, please?
B Yes, sure. Where do you want to sit?
A In the center, please.
B OK. That's $ ³___.
A Here you are.
B $ ⁴___. Thank you. Here are your tickets and $ ⁵___ change.
A Which screen is it, please?
B It's screen ⁶___.
A Thanks.

You ask	You answer
What time is the next showing of …?	It's at 8 p.m.
Can I have … tickets, please?	Yes, sure. That's $22.
Where do you want to sit?	In the center.
Which screen is it?	It's screen 4.

2 🔘 **Pronunciation** /s/, /k/, **and** /tʃ/ **Listen and repeat.**

/s/	center	cent
/k/	ticket	screen
/tʃ/	change	children

3 🔘 **Listen and choose the correct answers.**

1 a /s/   b /k/   c /tʃ/
2 a /s/   b /k/   c /tʃ/
3 a /s/   b /k/   c /tʃ/

4 Pairwork Write and practice dialogues. 🎭

1 Buy three tickets for *Harry Potter and the Deathly Hallows*. The tickets cost $12 each. Ask for seats in the center. Pay with a $50 note. Ask which screen it's on (screen 5) and the time of the next showing (8 p.m.).

2 Buy two tickets for *Fantastic Mr. Fox*. Ask for seats in the center. The tickets cost $13 each. Pay with a $20 note. Ask the time of the next showing (7:45 p.m.) and which screen it's on (screen 3).

Grammar

Simple past
Interrogative and short answers

Interrogative		
Did	I / you / he / she / it / we / you / they	go?
Short answers		
Yes,	I / you / he / she / it / we / you / they	did.
No,		didn't.

Rules p.W20

1 **Write simple past questions and short answers.**

Rob / play tennis / yesterday? (✓)
Did Rob play tennis yesterday? Yes, he did.

1 Louise / make a pizza / on the weekend? (✗)
2 Danny / buy a sweatshirt / on Saturday morning? (✓)
3 Neil and Sarah / watch a horror movie / last night? (✗)
4 Sofia / go / to school yesterday? (✗)
5 the team / win the game? (✓)

Question words + Simple past

Question word	*did*	Subject	Main verb?
What	did	they	do?
Where	did	you	go?
Who	did	he	talk with?
Why	did	she	run?

Rules p.W21

2 **Complete the interview. Use the simple past form of the verbs.**

Q <u>Why did you buy</u> (why / you / buy) tickets for the premiere of *Transformers* in Tokyo?
A I ¹_____ (not buy) them! I ²_____ (win) them in a competition on TV! The prize ³_____ (be) a trip to Tokyo and two tickets to the premiere!

Q ⁴_____ (who / you / give) the other ticket to?
A I ⁵_____ (give) it to my dad. He ⁶_____ (love) *Transformers* when he ⁷_____ (be) a child!
Q ⁸_____ (what / you / do) in Tokyo?
A Oh, we ⁹_____ (have) a fantastic time! We ¹⁰_____ (not stay) very long – only four days, but we ¹¹_____ (see) a lot of the city.
Q What about the movie? ¹²_____ (you / like) it?
A Yes, I ¹³_____. I ¹⁴_____ (love) it!
Q ¹⁵_____ (you / meet) any of the stars?
A No, I ¹⁶_____. I ¹⁷_____ (want) to get Shia LaBeouf's autograph and I ¹⁸_____ (wait) outside the movie theater, but I ¹⁹_____ (not see) him. I think he ²⁰_____ (leave) early.

3 **Game! Question time.**

Divide into teams. Use the words below to write simple past questions.

You have 3 minutes!

Ask one person in a different team each question.

Team A   What did you do yesterday?
          (= 1 point for Team A)
Team B   I went to school.
          (= 1 point for Team B)

What	do	on vacation
Why	eat	yesterday
Who	finish	last night
Where	get	on your birthday
What time	meet	last year
	go	
	see	
	start	
	study	
	watch	

Finished?

Write five simple past questions for your partner.

What did you eat for lunch yesterday?
When did you ...?

CD-ROM ▶ Workbook p.W23

Shia LaBeouf – a new star in Hollywood!

Shia LaBeouf (6/11/86) is an American actor and comedian. He starred in the Transformers *movies and acted with Harrison Ford in* Indiana Jones and the Kingdom of the Crystal Skull. *He's one of the best young actors in Hollywood.*

We talked to movie critic, Martin Metzler, about Shia's life and success.

Question 1 _____

Martin Well, Shia comes from a family of performers and he was very young when he started to act. He was a TV actor when he was only twelve years old and he appeared in popular TV shows, such as *The X-Files*.

Question 2 _____

Martin He became famous in 2000 when he played the part of Louis Stevens on the Disney series *Even Stevens*. The show was about the life of the Stevens family and Shia was one of the children in the family. He did very well – he won an Emmy award for his performance!

Question 3 _____

Martin Shia made his movie debut in 2003 in a movie called *Holes*. Steven Spielberg saw the movie and thought he was really good. He offered him the part of Sam Witwicky in his new movie, *Transformers*. The movie was a success and Shia became a world famous movie star!

Question 4 _____

Martin There isn't a secret. He's just a great actor and a natural comedian. He's the best!

Reading

1 Read the text. Complete the interview with the missing questions.

- When did he become famous?
- When did Shia start to act?
- What's the secret of Shia's success?
- When did he have his first movie role?

2 Read the text again. Answer the questions.

When was Shia LaBeouf born? *He was born on June 11ᵗʰ, 1986.*

1 What TV show did he appear in when he was twelve?
2 What part did he play in the Disney series *Even Stevens*?
3 What did he win for his performance in the series?
4 Why did Steven Spielberg offer Shia a part in the movie *Transformers*?

Listening

3 **Listen to two teenagers discussing a movie. Choose the correct answers.**

Mike had a good / bad weekend. He went to the movies on ¹Saturday / Sunday. His friend ²Kate / Kevin didn't want to go because ³he / she was tired, so he went with ⁴Kate / Kevin. They saw ⁵*The Lightning Thief* / *Tooth Fairy*. Mike's friend ⁶didn't like / quite liked the movie, but Mike ⁷liked / loved it. He thought the child actors in the movie were ⁸awful / fantastic.

Speaking

4 **Think of a movie you saw last year. Then complete the chart.**

Title	
Kind of movie	
Actors in the movie	
Your opinion of the actors	
Your opinion of the movie	

5 **Pairwork Discuss the movies you watched. Ask and answer questions.**

- What movie / you / watch?
- Who / be / the stars of the movie?
- What / you / think of the actors?
- What / you / think of the movie?

Writing

6 **Write a short text about two movies. Choose a movie you really liked and a movie you didn't like. Write about …**

- the name of the movie
- the kind of movie it is
- when and where you saw it
- who you were with
- your opinion of the actors
- your opinion of the movie

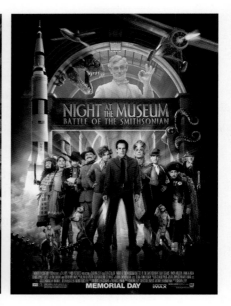

CD-ROM ▸ Workbook p. W25

Vocabulary

1 Complete the job words.

teacher

1 p_____
w_____

2 d_____

3 l_____

4 a_____

5 j_____

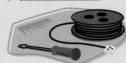

6 e_____

7 h_____

8 e_____

9 s_____

2 Read the descriptions and write the movie types.

A cartoon *animated movie*

1 A movie about life and travel in the future _____

2 A movie about a fictional world or parallel world _____

3 A fast and exciting movie _____

4 A funny movie with a simple plot _____

5 A romantic movie about love _____

6 A very frightening movie _____

Grammar

3 Complete the sentences with the simple past form of the verbs in the box.

| ~~call~~ | do | give | prefer | sing |
| stay | stop | think | watch | |

She *called* her mom because she was late.

1 The car _____ in front of the house.

2 I _____ Sam was your brother.

3 I _____ the blue T-shirt to the red T-shirt.

4 Fanny Lú _____ all her hits at the concert.

5 Ana _____ her homework yesterday.

6 They _____ in a very nice hotel.

7 We _____ the baseball game at Alberto's house.

8 Elena _____ me an MP3 player for my birthday.

4 Complete the postcard with the simple past of the verbs.

Hello from San Francisco!

Yesterday morning, we <u>went</u> (go) on a bus tour of the city. It ¹_____ (be) fantastic! We ²_____ (see) the Golden Gate Bridge, the City Hall, and Fisherman's Wharf. We ³_____ (have) lunch at Fisherman's Wharf and then ⁴_____ (walk) around the shopping center. I ⁵_____ (buy) some cool souvenirs! In the afternoon, we ⁶_____ (get) a ferry to Alcatraz. It's a famous prison on an island near the city. Dad ⁷_____ (take) a photo of me in a prison cell! In the evening we ⁸_____ (visit) the Chinatown area of San Francisco and I ⁹_____ (try) Chinese food for the first time. It ¹⁰_____ (be) really good!

See you soon,

Miriam

5 Rewrite the sentences with the negative form of the simple past.

Miko won the karaoke competition.
Miko didn't win the karaoke competition.

1 We saw *Land of the Lost* last night.

2 I invited Marco to the party.

3 Lucy spent a lot of money on vacation.

4 Abel thought the movie was good.

5 Mom told me to do my homework.

6 Write questions and short answers.

Mateus / watch a movie / last night? (✗)
<u>Did Mateus watch a movie last night?</u>
<u>No, he didn't.</u>

1 Ellen / learn to play the piano / at school? (✓)

_____
_____

2 your parents / meet after work? (✗)

_____
_____

3 you / see *Valentine's Day*? (✗)

_____
_____

4 the postal worker / deliver a letter for me? (✓)

_____
_____

5 the electrician / come this morning? (✗)

_____
_____

7 Complete the dialogue with the simple past form of the verbs or short answers.

Sandro <u>Did you go</u> (you / go) to the movies with Isabel yesterday?

Pedro No, I ¹_____. We agreed to meet but she didn't come.

Sandro Really? ²_____ (she / call) you to explain?

Pedro No, she ³_____. I waited forty minutes! I was really mad!

Sandro ⁴_____ (what / you / do)?
⁵_____ (you / go) home?

Pedro No, I ⁶_____. I saw Natalia and Ruben outside the movie theater.

Sandro So, ⁷_____ (you / watch) the movie with them?

Pedro Yes, ⁸_____. We saw *G.I. Joe*.

Sandro ⁹_____ (you / like) it?

Pedro Yes, ¹⁰_____. It was great.

Sandro ¹¹_____ (what / Natalia and Ruben / think) of it?

Pedro Well, Ruben loved it, but Natalia hated it. She wanted to see *Hannah Montana The Movie*.

Sandro Typical! What about Isabel?
¹²_____ (she / arrive) in the end?

Pedro No, ¹³_____ but she called me this morning.

Sandro ¹⁴_____ (what / she / say)?
¹⁵_____ (she / apologize)?

Pedro Yes, ¹⁶_____, but I'm still mad!

Got it?

8 Sara had an audition for a part in a movie. Complete her blog with the simple past form of the verbs.

My Blog

Last week, I <u>went</u> (go) to the auditions for a part in a movie.
I ¹_____ (travel) to Hollywood the night before the auditions with my mom and my friend Sophie. We ²_____ (wait) outside the studio all night and we ³_____ (not sleep). It was so exciting! The auditions ⁴_____ (start) at about nine o'clock. At first, we ⁵_____ (go) into a room with some other girls and we ⁶_____ (say) our names and ⁷_____ (tell) the people where we were from. After that, the movie people ⁸_____ (ask) Sophie and I to go into a different room. We ⁹_____ (not know) at the time, but that ¹⁰_____ (be) the first selection! The other girls ¹¹_____ (not have) an audition. I ¹²_____ (not do) very well because I was nervous. I ¹³_____ (not get) the part, but I ¹⁴_____ (have) a great day!

9 Write the questions. Then write the answers.

What / Sara / audition for?
<u>What did Sara audition for? She auditioned</u>
<u>for a part in a movie.</u>

1 Sara / travel to Hollywood?

_____

2 Who / she / go with?

_____

3 Where / they wait / all night?

_____

4 What time / the auditions / start?

_____

5 Sara and Sophie / know about / the first audition?

_____

6 How / Sara / do in her audition?

_____

It all started with a mouse!

Today, the Walt Disney Company is very big. It has movie studios, TV channels, movie theaters, and theme parks. But in the 1920s it was very small. That changed when Walt Disney created a little cartoon mouse. He called the mouse Mortimer, but his wife, Lillian, didn't like the name and she suggested Mickey.

Mickey appeared in the cartoon, *Plane Crazy*, in 1928. People liked the movie, but the Hollywood movie studios didn't want to buy it because it was a silent movie and the characters didn't talk in it. Soon Mickey started to talk in his cartoons and he became a star. At first,

Walt Disney did the voices of Mickey and his girlfriend, Minnie. Mickey had a funny voice and people loved it! They also loved his clothes: yellow shoes, red shorts, and white gloves.

In 1955, Mickey was on a TV program, the *Mickey Mouse Club*. The *Mickey Mouse Club* became a popular children's TV show in America. It had news, animated movies, and music. Britney Spears, Justin Timberlake, and Christina Aguilera started their careers on the show.

Today, people still love Mickey Mouse. He's the symbol of the Walt Disney Company because Walt Disney never forgot that "it all started with a mouse!"

1 Before you read **What do you know about Mickey Mouse? Do the quiz. Then read the text and check your answers.**

1 Who created Mickey Mouse?	a Joseph Barbera	b Walt Disney
2 What was Mickey's original name?	a Oswald	b Mortimer
3 When did he first star in a cartoon?	a 1928	b 1950
4 What color are Mickey's shorts?	a yellow	b red
5 Who is Mickey's girlfriend?	a Minnie	b Millie

2 Read the text again. Complete the sentences with the missing information.

In the 1920s, Walt Disney created Mickey Mouse.
1 Mickey's first cartoon was _____. Walt Disney made it in _____.
2 It wasn't a success because _____.
3 Soon Mickey _____ in his cartoons.
4 People loved Mickey's _____ voice and his _____.
5 In 1955, Mickey appeared on _____. It was called _____.
6 Today people still _____.

3 Focus on you **Use the questions below to talk about your favorite animated characters. Then prepare a short oral presentation.**

1 What was your favorite animated character when you were a child?
2 What animated movie / TV show did it appear in?
3 Why did you like it?

My progress

Speaking and writing

1 **I can write and talk about famous sports personalities.**   **A2**

Michael Jordan played basketball.

1 _____
2 _____
3 _____
4 _____
5 _____

Got it? ____ / 5

2 **I can identify different jobs.**   **A2**

hairdresser

1 _____
2 _____
3 _____
4 _____
5 _____

Got it? ____ / 5

3 **I can apologize and make excuses.**   **A2**

I'm sorry.

1 _____
2 _____
3 _____
4 _____
5 _____

Got it? ____ / 5

4 **I can invent a story in the past.**   **A2**

Last year, I met a famous person.

1 _____
2 _____
3 _____
4 _____
5 _____

Got it? ____ / 5

5 **I can ask and answer questions about past activities.**   **A2**

What did you do yesterday?

1 _____
2 _____
3 _____
4 _____
5 _____

Got it? ____ / 5

6 **I can buy a movie ticket.**   **A2**

Can I have two tickets, please.

1 _____
2 _____
3 _____
4 _____
5 _____

Got it? ____ / 5

Reading, listening, and writing

		Got It?	
	Yes	I'm not sure	No
7 I can write and summarize facts about a famous person. A2	☐	☐	☐
8 I can read and understand a text about a Hollywood star. A2	☐	☐	☐
9 I can identify and describe different kinds of movies. A2	☐	☐	☐
10 I can write about movies I liked / disliked. A2	☐	☐	☐

Remember

Vocabulary

1 **Match the words in columns A and B. Then write the words in the chart.**

A	B
wavy	story
classical	worker
rock 'n'	guitarist
postal	hair
sales	eyes
love	roll
green	movie
horror	clerk

Physical descriptions	Music	Jobs	Movies
wavy hair	2_____	4_____	6_____
1_____	3_____	5_____	7_____

2 **How many more words can you add to the categories in the chart in two minutes?**

1 = Not very good   2 = OK   3 = Good
4 = Very good   5 = Excellent!

Grammar

Simple present and present progressive

3 **Complete the dialogues with the correct forms of the present simple or the present progressive tense.**

1
A Where's Natalia? ¹_____ (she / do) her homework?
B No, she ²_____. She ³_____ (never / do) her homework in the afternoon. She's in the living room with Katie. They ⁴_____ (watch) a movie.

2
A What ¹_____ (you / do) in your free time?
B I'm in a band. I ²_____ (play) the drums.
A Where ³_____ (your band / play)?
B In my house! We ⁴_____ (not be) very good, but we ⁵_____ (practice) every day!

3
A What kind of music ¹_____ (you / like)?
B I ²_____ (not / like) music but I like books. I ³_____ (read) every day.
A What book ⁴_____ (you / read) right now?
B I ⁵_____ (read) a book by R.L. Stine.
A ⁶_____ (he / write) love stories?
B No, he ⁷_____. He ⁸_____ (write) horror stories!

Possessive pronouns

4 **Complete the sentences with the correct possessive pronoun.**

My sister doesn't have an MP3 player, so she always uses m*ine*.

1 Your classroom is fantastic! O_____ is terrible!
2 Whose pen is this? Is it y_____?
3 "Is that Mia's cat?" "No, h_____ is black."
4 This isn't my English book. M_____ has my name in it.
5 Give this ball to the boys. It's t_____.
6 His name is Jack and h_____ is Vanessa.

Adverbs

5 **Complete the sentences with the adverb form of the adjectives.**

My grandma drives *slowly*. (slow)

1 Scott plays the piano _____. (beautiful)
2 I like his books. He writes _____. (good)
3 She's a great actor, but she sings _____. (bad)
4 I can't understand Amy. She speaks _____. (fast)
5 The students are working _____. (quiet)
6 You paint _____. (fantastic)

Simple past

6 Match the base forms of the irregular verbs with their simple past forms.

1(o) be – was / were

1	be	a	made
2	**come**	b	**had**
3	**do**	c	**ate**
4	drink	d	wrote
5	**eat**	e	**read**
6	*get*	f	*spoke*
7	**give**	g	WENT
8	GO	h	**gave**
9	have	i	left
10	**leave**	j	came
11	make	k	did
12	**read**	l	**saw**
13	ride	m	won
14	run	n	ran
15	see	o	was / were
16	speak	p	got
17	spend	q	rode
18	take	r	drank
19	win	s	spent
20	**write**	t	**took**

7 Complete the message with the simple past forms of the verbs.

Hi, Sal

Yesterday, it <u>was</u> (be) my birthday. I ¹_____ (have) a fantastic day. I ²_____ (not go) to school and I ³_____ (not get up) early – it was Saturday!

I ⁴_____ (get up) at 9 o'clock and my parents ⁵_____ (make) me a special breakfast! Then my parents ⁶_____ (give) me an MP3 player.

I ⁷_____ (spend) the morning with my friends. They ⁸_____ (come) to my house and we ⁹_____ (read) magazines and ¹⁰_____ (listen) to music.

In the evening, I ¹¹_____ (go) to Pizza Pizza – my favorite Italian restaurant. All my friends ¹²_____ (be) there. We ¹³_____ (eat) pizzas and ¹⁴_____ (drink) cola. We ¹⁵_____ (have) a great time!

Then, we went to the movies! We ¹⁶_____ (see) *Star Trek*. I got home at 10:30 and ¹⁷_____ (speak) with my parents about the movie. I went to bed at 11:30!

¹⁸_____ (what / you / do) yesterday? Did you have a good day, too?

Write soon!

Kylie

5 Is Sam playing?

Check it out!

two o'clock sharp

1 🔘 Read and listen Who is the new team captain?

a Teo **b** Justin **c** Sam

CC	Quiet! Do you have any questions about the game on Saturday?
Joe	Where are we meeting?
CC	We're meeting at the school at one thirty.
Dylan	How are we getting to Riverfield?
CC	We're taking the school bus.
Adam	What time is it leaving?
CC	It's leaving at two o'clock sharp so don't be late.
Adam	How long does it take to get there?
CC	It takes about an hour.
Teo	Is Sam playing?
CC	No, he isn't. Justin is taking his place. He's the new team captain.
Teo	What?
Sam	Sorry I'm late, Coach. What are the plans for Saturday?
CC	You're not playing, Sam.
Sam	What?
CC	You did badly in the math test on Wednesday. You're off the team.

2 Comprehension Use the information in the dialogue to complete Coach Carson's information sheet.

Westside Basketball vs Riverfield Rockets.

Date of game: Saturday, November 12th

Meeting place: _____.

Transportation: _____.

Departure time: _____ sharp!

Language focus

3 Dialogue focus Complete the dialogues with questions and answers.

Joe Where / meeting?
Where are we meeting?

CC 1 _____

Dylan How / getting to Riverfield?
2 _____

CC 3 _____

Adam What time / leaving?
4 _____

CC 5 _____

Teo Sam / playing?
6 _____

CC 7 _____

4 💿 **Listen and check. Then listen and repeat.**

5 Focus on you Read the dialogue. Then write three similar dialogues with the information below.

Time: 2:30 p.m.
Place: at school.

Time: 7 p.m.
Place: in front of the movie theater

Time: 11:15 a.m.
Place: at the bus stop

Time: 8:30 p.m.
Place: at Gino's Pizzeria.

A What time are we meeting?
B We're meeting at *2:30 p.m.*
A Where are we meeting?
B We're meeting *at school.*

6 Pairwork Practice the dialogues in exercise 5.

Transportation

1 **Match the pictures with the kinds of transportation.**

airplane   bike   boat   bus   ~~car~~   ferry   helicopter
motorcycle   subway   taxi   train   truck

car _____

Look!

• *by car*
• *by train*
• *by bike*
but
• *on foot*

2 🔘 **Listen and check. Then listen and repeat.**

3 **Pairwork** **Ask and answer questions about how you and your family go to work or school.** 🎭

by car   catch the train   drive   ride a bike
take a bus   take the subway   walk

A How do you come to school?
B I usually take the bus, but I sometimes walk.

A How does your mom / dad go to work?
B He / She drives.

Present progressive for future

Think!

- **Read the sentences. Then complete the rule with an expression from the box.**

Where are we meeting?
We're meeting at the school at two o'clock.

> future plans   habitual actions   past events

- We use the present progressive to talk about _____ especially when we mention a time and / or place.

Rules p.W26

Future time expressions

this morning / afternoon / evening / week
tonight
on Tuesday / Wednesday / November 1st
tomorrow
tomorrow morning / afternoon / evening / night
next Friday / week / weekend / month / year
in July / the summer / 2012
at Christmas / Easter / six o'clock

Rules p.W26

1 **Look at Robert's dayplanner. Rewrite the sentences with true information.**

Monday:	study math with Jane.
Tuesday:	play tennis with Alison
Wednesday:	visit my grandparents in the afternoon
Thursday:	finish my science project
Friday:	have pizza with Ben and Jake
Saturday:	watch the baseball game at John's house
Sunday:	go skateboarding with Seb

On Monday, Robert is studying with Seb.
He isn't studying with Seb.
He's studying math with Jane.

1 Robert's having a piano lesson on Tuesday.
2 He's visiting his grandparents on Wednesday evening.
3 He's starting his history project on Thursday.
4 He's staying at home on Friday evening.
5 He's playing a basketball game on Saturday.
6 He's going swimming with Seb on Sunday.

2 **Complete the dayplanner with information about you. Then write sentences.**

Monday	Have lunch with _____.
Tuesday	Play basketball with _____.
Wednesday	Visit my _____.
Thursday	Finish my _____ project.
Friday	Go to _____'s house to study for _____ test.
Saturday	Buy new _____ CD.
Sunday	Go to the movies to see _____.

3 **Choose the correct answers.**

My parents are going to Rome on (Friday) / July.

1 I'm meeting Harry this **evening** / **tonight**.
2 I'm playing chess with Oscar tomorrow **week** / **afternoon**.
3 What are you doing next **afternoon** / **Monday**?
4 Alice is having her birthday party on **October 5th** / **June**.
5 She isn't going to the movies this **night** / **evening**.
6 Are you studying for the math test **tomorrow** / **afternoon**?

Finished?

Choose five future time expressions and say what your plans are.

At Christmas: I'm visiting my grandparents in Hawaii at Christmas.

Communication

Making arrangements

1 🔘 **Read and listen to the dialogue. Choose the correct answers.**
Listen and check. Then listen and repeat.

Sarah	Hi, Olivia. Are you free tomorrow evening?
Olivia	Yes, I am. / (No, I'm not.) I'm seeing Kate tomorrow, but I'm free on Tuesday evening.
Sarah	Great. Let's do something together on Tuesday, then.
Olivia	Good idea. What do you want to do?
Sarah	How about ¹going to the movies / watching a DVD?

Olivia	There aren't any good movies on at the moment. Why don't we ²go bowling / go swimming, instead?
Sarah	That's a great idea. Let's meet in front of ³my house / the bus stop.
Olivia	OK. At what time? How long does it take to get there?
Sarah	It takes about ⁴30 / 40 minutes. Is ⁵seven / eight thirty OK?
Olivia	Yes, that's fine. See you then.

You say	You answer
Are you free on …?	Yes, I am. / No, I'm not.
What do you want to do?	Let's go / do / play … Why don't we go / do / play …
How about going to the park?	Yes. / OK. / All right / Good idea. No. / No, I'm sorry. I can't. / No, I don't like …
Let's meet at …	Is seven thirty OK?
At what time?	

2 🔘 **Pronunciation** /oʊ/ **and** /u/ **Listen and repeat.**

/oʊ/ Let's go swimming.
/u/ What do you want to do?

3 🔘 **Listen to the conversations. Answer the questions.**

* What do they decide to do?
* Where do they decide to meet?
* What time do they decide to meet?

1 Activity: _They're going bowling._
  Place: _____
  Time: _____

2 Activity: _____
  Place: _____
  Time: _____

3 Activity: _____
  Place: _____
  Time: _____

4 Pairwork **Make arrangements with your partner. Accept or refuse suggestions from the box. Then decide on a time and a place to meet.** 🎭

> do your homework together   go bowling   go cycling
> go for a walk   go swimming   go to a baseball game
> play video games   surf the Internet

How long …? + take

Think!

Read the sentences. Then complete the rule with *How long*, *takes*, and *take*.

How long does it take you to get to school? It takes about an hour.

• ¹_____ does it + ²_____ + (*you*) + infinitive of the verb with *to*?
It + ³_____ + length of time.

Rules p.W27

1 Write questions and answers.

How long / travel / from Los Angeles to San Francisco by bus? (six hours)
How long does it take to travel from Los Angeles to San Francisco by bus?
It takes six hours.

1 How long / fly from Miami to Atlanta? (two hours)
2 How long / you / have breakfast? (15 minutes)
3 How long / go to the Statue of Liberty by ferry? (1 hour)
4 How long / you / take a shower? (5 minutes)
5 How long / you / do your homework? (2 hours)
6 How long / you / go to school? (20 minutes)

2 Complete the e-mail with the correct forms of the verbs in the box.

| come | do | go | go | have | meet |
| organize | take | travel | ~~visit~~ | watch |

Hi, Airton
How are you? I'm really excited because next weekend I'm visiting my cousins Josh and Jenny in Boston. I ¹_____ with my mom.
We ²_____ the nine o'clock train from New Haven. The journey takes two hours and ten minutes. We ³_____ my cousins and Aunt Rachel outside Boston South Station. On Saturday afternoon, we ⁴_____ shopping downtown.
We ⁵_____ lunch in the Fenway district.
On Saturday evening, Jenny and I ⁶_____ Josh play a very important volleyball game. Josh's birthday is on Sunday. We ⁷_____ a surprise party for him! All his friends ⁸_____.
What ⁹_____ you _____ next weekend? Are you going to see Rodrigo in Brasília?
How long does it take you to ¹⁰_____ there from Belo Horizonte?
Write soon,
Laura

3 Game! Make plans for a vacation. Use as many words from the chart as you can.

airplane	go shopping	Chicago	2 days
bike	go swimming	Los Angeles	3 hours
bus	go to the movies	Miami	5 hours
car	have dinner	New Orleans	7 hours
ferry	meet friends	New York	8 p.m
subway	play sports	Orlando	10 days
train	visit museums	San Diego	12 p.m.

Next week, I'm going on vacation to San Diego. We're traveling by airplane. It takes …

Finished?

Write five questions for your partner with *How long does it take you …?*

How long does it take you to get to school?

Skateboarder conquers Australia

David Cornthwaite was the first man to travel across Australia on a skateboard! The 5,823 km journey took him five months to complete. He skateboarded from Perth on the west coast to Brisbane on the east coast.

"I skated about 50 kilometers every day. The middle of the day was very hot, so I usually skated in the morning and evening."

David traveled with seven other people. One person followed him on a bike – the others traveled behind in two jeeps. They helped him when he had problems. And there were lots of problems! Sometimes it was very dangerous. "Some of the trucks on the road are enormous and very dangerous!"

Animals were also a problem. David saw some very big snakes and lots of dogs chased him! "One day I had a race with an emu! It was a very big bird and it ran very fast but I won the race!"

He also had terrible problems with his feet. "I used 13 pairs of shoes! I was in constant pain and I felt like an old man!"

So why did he do it? He wanted to raise money for children's charities in Australia. "People were very generous. I made $80,000 for charity."

Reading

1 Answer the questions.

How long did it take David to cross Australia on his skateboard?
It took David five months to travel across Australia.

1 How many kilometers did he skate every day?
2 How many people traveled with him?
3 What animals did he meet?
4 How many pairs of shoes did he use?
5 How much money did he make for charity?

Listening

2 💿 **Listen to the interview with skateboarder Greg Fisher. Are the sentences true or false? Then listen again and correct the false statements.**

Greg is a champion rollerskater. *False. Greg is champion skateboarder.*
1 Greg is planning to skate across Africa.
2 He's leaving on June 12th.
3 He's traveling with his dad and his two brothers.
4 Greg is sleeping on a school bus.
5 He's going to Seattle, Washington first.
6 His final destination is Springfield, Virginia.
7 He's hoping to get to the east coast at the beginning of August.
8 He's collecting money for charity.

Speaking

3 **Pairwork** **Complete the factfile. Ask your partner about the trip he / she is planning.** 🎭

Destination San Diego
Traveling with _____
Departure date _____
Transportation _____
Length of journey _____
Accommodation Hotel near the California Tower
Number of days 3

Activities
• Day 1 – Visit the Old Town and Balboa Park
• Day 2 – Spend the day at Sea World.
• Day 3 – Take a boat trip in San Diego Harbor

- where / go?
- who / go with?
- when / leave?
- how / get there?
- how long / journey / take?

- how long / stay?
- where / stay?
- what / do / first day?
- what / do / second day?
- what / do / third day?

A Where are you going?
B We're going to San Diego.

Writing

4 **Complete the e-mail with the information about you from exercise 3.**

Hi, Lola
Great news! I'm going on a short vacation to <u>San Diego</u>. I'm going with
1_____. We 2_____ on July 10th. We're traveling by 3_____. We're
staying in 4_____. On the first day, we 5_____ the Old Town and Balboa
Park. On the second day, we 6_____ the day at Sea World. I want to see
Shamu, the killer whale. On the third day, we 7_____ a boat trip in San Diego
Harbor. It's my first visit to San Diego and I'm so excited! Are you going on vacation?
Love,
Kate

5 **Imagine you are planning a trip. Write an e-mail about your plans.**

Are there any tomatoes?

Check it out!

Yuck!	Just a couple.
Yum!	How come?
Very funny	

1 Read and listen What is Zoe making?

a a pizza   b sandwiches   c a cake

Teo I'm hungry. Is there any food in the refrigerator, Zoe?

Zoe I don't know. Let me see. Yes, there is, but there isn't much. There's some ham. Would you like a ham sandwich?

Teo Yes, OK. Are there any tomatoes?

Zoe No, there aren't. There's a lot of lettuce.

Teo Yuck! I hate lettuce. Is there any cheese?

Zoe No, there isn't. There are some carrots, but there aren't many.

Teo Yum … a ham and carrot sandwich! My favorite!

Zoe Very funny, Teo. Anyway, how many ham sandwiches do you want?

Teo Just a couple. What about you, Sam?

Sam No, not for me, thanks. I'm not hungry.

Zoe You aren't hungry! How come?

Teo He got a bad mark in the math test. He's off the basketball team.

Sam It isn't fair!

Teo Oh, stop moaning Sam! Just study and get a good report card!

Sam It isn't that easy, Teo.

Zoe Can I help you? I like studying.

Teo Yes! That's a great idea. Zoe's brilliant.

Sam Thanks, Zoe. I really want to play in the basketball championship.

2 Comprehension Answer the questions.

How does Teo feel? *Teo is hungry.*

1 What does Zoe offer Teo to eat?
2 Why is Sam not hungry?
3 How does Zoe offer to help Sam?

Language focus

3 Dialogue focus Write the sentences and questions in the correct order.

1 Teo I'm hungry.
Zoe / any / is / refrigerator / there / in / the / food
<u>Is there any food in the refrigerator, Zoe?</u>

Zoe I don't know. Let me see. Yes, there is, much / there / but / isn't /
1 _____.

There's some ham. like / you / a / sandwich / ham / would
2 _____?

Teo Yes, OK.

2 Teo any / are / tomatoes / there
3 _____?

Zoe No, there aren't.
lettuce / a lot of / there's
4 _____.

Teo Yuck! I hate lettuce.
cheese / is / any / there
5 _____?

Zoe No, there isn't.
carrots / there / some / are / many / aren't / there / but
6 _____.

3 Zoe sandwiches / you / how / ham / want / many / do / anyway
7 _____?

Teo Just a couple.
you / about / Sam / what
8 _____?

Sam thanks / not / me / no / for
9 _____.

I'm not hungry.

4 Listen and check. Then listen and repeat.

5 Focus on you Work in groups of three. Use the food in the box to write dialogues.

an apple   a hamburger   an orange   ~~a sandwich~~

A I'm hungry.
B Would you like <u>a sandwich</u>?
A Yeah, OK.

B What about you, (*Alberto*)?
C No, not for me, thanks.

6 Group work In groups of three practice the dialogues in exercise 5.

Vocabulary

Food and drink

1 Match the words with the pictures.

apple   beef   bread   carrot   cheese   chicken   cookie   egg
mango   milk   orange juice   potato   rice   salmon
tomato   ~~tuna~~   water   yogurt

tuna

2 Listen and check. Then listen and repeat.

3 Copy the chart into your exercise book. Complete it with the food words from exercise 1. Add any other food words you know.

Fruit	Vegetables	Meat	Fish	Dairy products	Drinks
apple	carrot	beef	salmon	yogurt	water

4 Pairwork Talk about the food and drink you like and don't like.

A What food do you like?
B I like pizza and chocolate.
A What food do you hate?
B I hate eggs and lettuce.
A What about drinks?
B I like cola, but I don't like coffee.

Look!

Animal	Meat
cow	*beef*
pig	*pork / ham*
sheep	*mutton*
but	
lamb	*lamb*
chicken	*chicken*
duck	*duck*

Grammar

Countable / Uncountable nouns

Countable		Uncountable
Singular	Plural	Singular only
an apple	apples	bread
a tomato	tomatoes	cheese

Think!

Complete the rules with *singular* and *plural*.

- Countable nouns can be [1]_____ or [2]_____.
- Uncountable nouns can only be [3]_____.

Rules p.W32

1 **Look at page 62. Complete the chart with five items for each category.**

Countable		Uncountable
Singular	Plural	Singular only
an egg	*eggs*	*milk*
1_____	6_____	11_____
2_____	7_____	12_____
3_____	8_____	13_____
4_____	9_____	14_____
5_____	10_____	15_____

some / any

	Countable		Uncountable
	Singular	Plural	Singular only
+	There's an apple.	There are some apples.	There's some bread.
-	There isn't an apple.	There aren't any apples.	There isn't any bread.
?	Is there an apple?	Are there any apples?	Is there any bread?

Think!

Complete the rules with *some* and *any*.

- We use [1]_____ with plural countable nouns and uncountable nouns in affirmative sentences.
- We use [2]_____ with plural countable nouns and uncountable nouns in negative sentences and questions.

Rules p.W32

2 **Choose the correct answers.**

Do you have **some** / **any** yogurt?
1 There aren't **some** / **any** eggs in the refrigerator.
2 Is there **any** / **a** milk in the bottle?
3 There is **some** / **any** cheese in the sandwich.
4 Are there **some** / **any** cookies on your desk?
5 There's **some** / **a** bread in the cupboard.

a lot of / much / many

	Countable	Uncountable
+	There are **a lot of** apples.	There's **a lot of** bread.
-	There aren't **many** apples.	There isn't **much** bread.
?	Are there **many** apples?	Is there **much** bread?

Think!

Choose the correct options.

In negative and interrogative sentences:
- *many* is used with [1]**countable / uncountable** nouns.
- *much* is used with [2]**countable / uncountable** nouns.

Rules p.W32

3 **Complete the sentences with *a lot of*, *much*, and *many*.**

My brother eats *a lot of* meat.
There aren't *many* tomatoes.
1 Luke likes _____ cheese in his sandwiches.
2 Do we need _____ eggs for this recipe?
3 You didn't buy _____ potatoes.
4 Karen eats _____ vegetables.
5 Are there _____ apples on the tree?
6 There isn't _____ water in the refrigerator.

4 **Game! What's in your refrigerator at home? Write down six items of food. Don't show your partner. Ask and answer questions to find out what is in your partner's refrigerator.**

A Is there any cheese?
B Yes, there is. (1 point!)
A Is there a lot of milk?
B No, there isn't. (0 points!)

Ordering food and drink

1 Read and listen to the dialogue. Complete the dialogue with words in the box. Listen and check. Then listen and repeat.

| ~~chicken~~ cookies orange juice potato soda tuna |

Server	How can I help you?
Mark	I'd like a _chicken_ sandwich, please.
Server	OK. What would you like to drink?
Mark	I'll have a ¹_____.
Server	Large or small?
Mark	Large, please.
Server	OK. And what about you? What would you like to eat?
Susan	I'd like a baked ²_____ with ³_____.
Server	OK. Would you like a drink?
Susan	Yes, please. I'll have an ⁴_____ and I'd like a few ⁵_____, too.
Server	OK. That's $15.75.

You ask	You answer
What would you like to eat / drink?	I'd like … / I'll have …
Would you like a … ?	Yes, please. / No, thanks.

2 **Pronunciation** Listen and repeat.

What would you like to eat?   Would you like a sandwich?
What would you like to drink?   Would you like a soda?

3 Listen to the conversations and complete the chart with the food and drink that the people order.

	Food	Drink
1		
2		
3		

4 Listen again and check.

5 **Group work** Work in groups of three. Look at the menu and order food and drink.

A How can I help you?
B I'd like …
A And would you like …?
B Yes, please. / No, thanks.
A OK. And what about you?
  What would you like to eat?
C I'll have …

Menu

Sandwiches:	cheese, chicken mayo, salmon	$4.20
Baked potatoes:	with cheese, tuna	$3.80
Burger and fries		$4.80
Carrot cake		$2.50
Fresh fruit:	apple, banana, mango	$0.80
Drinks:	coffee	$2.10
	tea	$1.75
	soda – small	$1.60
	– large	$2.40
	orange juice	$2.30
	water	$1.10

Grammar

How much ...? / How many ...?

Countable	Uncountable
How many sandwiches do you want?	**How much** milk is there?

Think!

- **Read the sentences. Then complete the rules with *how much* and *how many*.**

  How much bread is there?
  How many carrots are there?
  - We use [1]_____ before countable nouns.
  - We use [2]_____ before uncountable nouns.

  Rules p.W33

1 **Look at the recipe for *Strawberry Milkshake*. Complete the questions with *How much ...? / How many ...?* Then answer the questions.**

Recipe

Strawberry Milkshake

For four people
500 grams of yogurt
12 large strawberries
100 grams of strawberry ice cream
1 orange

<u>How much</u> yogurt is there in the recipe?
<u>There are 500 grams of yogurt.</u>

1 _____ strawberries are there?
_____

2 _____ strawberry ice cream is there?
_____

3 _____ oranges are there?
_____

4 _____ people is the recipe for?
_____

a little / a few

Think!

- **Read the sentences. Then choose the correct word.**

  There's a little yogurt.
  There are a few carrots.
  - We use *a little* with [1]**countable / uncountable** nouns.
  - We use *a few* with [2]**countable / uncountable** nouns.

  Rules p.W33

2 **Complete the sentences with *a little* or *a few*.**

We need <u>a few</u> eggs for this recipe.
1 I drink tea with _____ milk.
2 There are _____ mangoes in the refrigerator.
3 Is there any cheese? Yes, but only _____.
4 I only want _____ potatoes.
5 There's only _____ bread. Can you buy some?
6 We ate _____ cookies because we were hungry.
7 I'd like strawberries with _____ chocolate ice cream.
8 He bought _____ cakes for his birthday party.

3 **Emma and her mom are writing a shopping list for a party. Choose the correct answers.**

Mom Emma, **how much /** (**how many**) people are coming to your party?

Emma Well, about twenty, I think.

Mom OK, so we need [1]**some / any** bread for sandwiches. [2]**How much / How many** bread do we have?

Emma We don't have [3]**much / many**. We need to buy [4]**some / any** bread. What about ham? [5]**How much / How many** ham is there in the refrigerator?

Mom Well, there's [6]**much / a lot of** ham, but only [7]**a little / a few** cheese. There are [8]**a lot of / many** tomatoes.

Emma OK. Orange juice. Is there [9]**some / any** orange juice?

Mom No, we need [10]**some / any** orange juice. And [11]**some / any** cookies. We can buy [12]**a few / a little** cookies.

Emma And [13]**any / a few** mangoes.

Mom Great. Let's go shopping!

Finished?

Write questions for your teacher with *How much ...?* and *How many ...?*

How much milk is in your refrigerator?
How many cookies do you eat every day?

Sam Stern:
Cooking up a storm!

1 Sam Stern is a famous chef, but he was already famous when he was fourteen years old! He's also the author of five cook books for teenagers, *Cooking Up a Storm*, *Real Food Real Fast*, *Get Cooking*, *Sam Stern's Student Cook Book,* and *Eat Vegetarian*. They show teenagers how to cook simple, healthy food for all situations – from a quick breakfast to a big Sunday dinner.

2 Sam thinks that teenagers don't have a very healthy diet. They eat a lot of fast food and they don't eat much fruit or many vegetables. He also thinks that young people don't cook much and he wants teenagers to spend more time in the kitchen and to have fun with food.

3 Sam lives at home with his parents, his three sisters, and his brother when he isn't at college. He often cooks for them. His favorite family dinner is roast chicken with roast potatoes and vegetables, and then chocolate mousse for dessert. He also loves Chinese food.

4 Sam isn't always in the kitchen, of course. He goes to college and in his free time he plays soccer, goes to the gym, listens to music, and watches TV. But cooking is his passion. He wants to be a food writer and own a restaurant when he leaves college.

Reading

1 Read the article. Match the topics with the paragraphs.

a information about Sam's family   paragraph _____
b Sam's opinion of teenage eating habits   paragraph _____
c information about Sam and his books   paragraph _____
d information about Sam's free-time activities   paragraph _____

2 Answer the questions.

When did Sam Stern become famous? *When he was fourteen years old.*
1 What does he think of teenagers' diets?
2 What is his favorite family meal?
3 What does he do in his free time?
4 What does he want to do when he leaves college?

Listening

3 Listen to two teenagers talking about the food they eat. Write down what they eat and drink. Then choose the correct options to describe their diets.

1 a Matt *chocolate* ...
   b Matt has a **healthy / unhealthy** diet.
2 a Molly *milk* ...
   b Molly has a **healthy / unhealthy** diet.

Speaking

4 Pairwork Ask your partner the questions in the food survey.

Teen scene: Healthy eating

Do you have a healthy diet or do you eat too much fast food? Answer our questions and find out!

1 How much water do you drink every day?
a no water
b not much water (*500ml*)
c a lot of water (*1–2 liters*)

2 How many portions of fruit and vegetables do you eat in a day?
a only one
b 2–3 portions
c 3–5 portions

3 How many times a week do you eat protein, for example meat, fish, chicken, or eggs?
a once or twice a week
b three or four times a week
c every day

4 How many times a week do you eat dairy products, for example milk and cheese?
a once or twice a week
b three or four times a week
c every day

5 How many times a week do you eat carbohydrates, for example bread, pasta, and potatoes?
a once or twice a week
b three or four times a week
c every day

6 How many cookies and candies do you eat in a day?
a a lot (*6–10*)
b not many (*3–5*)
c one or two

Calculate your score: a = 0 points b = 1 point c = 2 points
Score:
11–16 Very good! You eat well! Keep it up!
6–10   OK. Your diet is quite healthy. What can you do to improve it?
0–5   You don't eat very well! Try to eat a healthy diet.

5 Tell the class about your partner's diet.

Maria has quite a healthy diet. She drinks a lot of water ...

Writing

6 Answer the questions. Write a short text about your diet.

- Do you have a healthy diet?
- How much fruit do you eat a day?
- How many times do you eat meat a week?
- How much candy do you eat a day?
- How many cookies and snacks do you eat a day?
- How much water do you drink a day?
- What can you cook?

Vocabulary

1 Complete the transportation words.

1 a i r p l a n e
2 h _ _ _ c _ _ _ _ r
3 b _ _
4 t _ _ i
5 t _ _ i _
6 b _ _ _
7 m _ _ _ _ _ _ c _ _
8 b _ _ t
9 f _ r _ _

2 Find ten more food words in the wordsearch.

o	r	a	n	g	e	j	b
c	m	p	c	s	g	u	s
h	i	p	h	b	g	i	l
i	l	l	e	r	i	c	e
c	k	e	e	e	l	e	p
k	f	i	s	t	u	n	a
e	b	r	e	a	d	j	f
n	d	w	a	t	e	r	d

Grammar

3 Write affirmative or negative sentences that are true for you. Use the present progressive form of the verbs in the box.

> do   get   ~~go~~   make   play
> take   visit

My friends and I _aren't going_ to the movies this evening.

1 My dad _____ dinner this evening.
2 I _____ my homework after school.
3 My mom _____ up early tomorrow morning.
4 I _____ a basketball game on Saturday.
5 My dad _____ a bus to work tomorrow.
6 I _____ my grandparents on the weekend.

4 Write questions and answers.

♥ ♥ ♥ ♥ ♥ **PUSSYCAT** dolls

Latin American Tour Dates

October 10th Monterrey, Mexico @ University Stadium 8 p.m.
October 12th São Paulo, Brazil @ Pacaembu Stadium 9 p.m.
October 13th Montevideo, Uruguay @ Estadio Centenario 8 p.m.
October 15th Santiago, Chile @ National Stadium 9 p.m.
October 18th Quito, Ecuador @ Coliseo General Ruminahui 9 p.m.
October 19th Buenos Aires, Argentina @ River Plate Stadium 9 p.m.

Where / the Pussycat Dolls tour / start?
Where is the Pussycat Dolls tour starting?
It's starting in Monterrey, Mexico.
1 How many / concerts / they / play / in Mexico?
2 When / Pussycat Dolls / play / in São Paulo?
3 Where / they / go / after São Paulo?
4 How many cities / they / visit / in Latin America?
5 How many concerts / they / do / in Latin America?
6 Where / the Pussycat Dolls / finish their tour?

5 Write the sentences in the correct order. Then order the events.

she / her / visiting / grandparents / is / this afternoon ☐1
She is visiting her grandparents this afternoon.
1 she / tomorrow / is / her friends / pizza / with / having / a / night ☐
2 tomorrow / is / she / playing / a / afternoon / game / volleyball ☐
3 is / Tracy's birthday party / going to / on the weekend / she ☐
4 she / next / in Phoenix / staying with her aunt / is / week ☐
5 with / Jane and Ann / is / studying / this / she / evening ☐

6 Write questions and give personal answers.

How long / get ready for school?
How long does it take you to get ready for school? It takes half an hour.
1 How long / do your homework?
2 How long / get to your grandparents' house?
3 How long / to read a book with 300 pages?
4 How long / take a shower?
5 How long / have your dinner?

7 Write the words in the box into the correct column.

> apple   bread   cookie   egg   milk
> orange juice   sandwich   water

Countable	Uncountable
apple	orange juice
1 _____	4 _____
2 _____	5 _____
3 _____	6 _____

8 Complete the sentences with *a*, *an*, *some*, or *any*.

There's **an** apple in my bag.

1 Are there _____ Spanish students in your school?
2 I have _____ egg for breakfast every morning.
3 Is that _____ apple or _____ mango?
4 I don't want _____ cheese on my burger.
5 There's _____ water on the table.
6 A Is there _____ fruit in the refrigerator?
   B Yes, there is. I bought _____ mangoes and _____ bananas yesterday.

9 Complete the questions with *How much ...?* or *How many ...?*

How much water do you drink every day?

1 _____ sugar do you put in your tea?
2 _____ apples did you buy?
3 _____ tomatoes are there?
4 _____ milk do you want?
5 _____ ham is there?
6 _____ eggs do you eat every week?

10 Choose the correct answers.

Do you want a little / a few milk in your coffee?

1 I don't eat **much** / **some** meat.
2 Do you drink **much** / **many** water?
3 There isn't **any** / **some** ham in this sandwich.
4 There's **a** / **some** bread in the cupboard.

Got it?

11 Choose the correct answers.

Alice   We **have** / **'re having** a surprise birthday party for Paul next Saturday. Can you come?
Jerry   Yeah. A surprise party. Cool! Where ¹**are you** / **you are** having it?
Alice   At my house on Hart Street. It only ²**is taking** / **takes** five minutes by bus from downtown.
Jerry   Great. What time is the party ³**starting** / **start**?
Alice   It's starting at eight o'clock.
Jerry   How ⁴**many** / **much** people are coming?
Alice   All the guys from the basketball team and ⁵**some** / **any** of Paul's school friends.
Jerry   Do you need ⁶**any** / **some** food or drink?
Alice   No, thanks. We have ⁷**a few** / **a lot of** food, but I don't have ⁸**much** / **many** CDs. Can you organize the music?
Jerry   Sure! No problem.

12 Answer the questions.

1 What is happening next Saturday?
   _____
2 How long does it take to get to Alice's house by bus?
   _____
3 What time is the party starting?
   _____
4 How much food does Alice have?
   _____
5 Does Alice have a lot of CDs?
   _____

The *Hard Rock Cafe* is the name of a very famous chain of restaurants. There are *Hard Rock Cafes* in London, New York, Paris, Tokyo, Rome, and a lot of other big cities in the world. In total, there are 135 *Hard Rock Cafes* in over 50 different countries!

The food at the *Hard Rock Cafe* is usually very good. Some of it is fast food, for example, burgers and fries, but you can also eat healthy food such as chicken, salmon, and salads, too.

But people don't go to a *Hard Rock Cafe* only for the food. They go for the music, too! There's always rock music and you can often listen to local rock bands and singers. A lot of *Hard Rock Cafes* are also rock museums.

The *Hard Rock Cafe* in New York, for example, has some of Elvis Presley's clothes and it also has some personal possessions from the Beatles, Nirvana, Madonna, and Gwen Stefani on its walls.

Hard Rock Cafes usually have a shop and tourists often buy *Hard Rock* T-shirts. Each T-shirt has the name of the city where the restaurant is. Some people travel to *Hard Rock Cafes* all over the world and buy a T-shirt in every restaurant!

1 Read the text. Then answer the questions.

1 How many *Hard Rock Cafes* are there in the world?
2 How many countries have *Hard Rock Cafes*?
3 What kind of food can you eat at the restaurants?
4 What kind of music can you hear at the restaurants?
5 What rock memorabilia is in the *Hard Rock Cafe* in New York?
6 What do tourists often buy at the restaurant shop?
7 What can you read on *Hard Rock* T-shirts?

2 Focus on you Write a short text about your favorite restaurant.

- What kind of restaurant is it? (fast food, pizzeria, Chinese …)
- Where is it?
- Who do you usually go with?
- What do you usually eat there?
- What do you like about it?

Speaking and writing

1 I can identify and talk about different types of transportation. **A2**

I take the bus to school.

1 _____
2 _____
3 _____
4 _____
5 _____

Got it? ____ / 5

2 I can talk about my future plans. **A2**

I'm going to New York on Friday.

1 _____
2 _____
3 _____
4 _____
5 _____

Got it? ____ / 5

3 I can make arrangements and accept or refuse suggestions. **A2**

Are you free tonight?

1 _____
2 _____
3 _____
4 _____
5 _____

Got it? ____ / 5

4 I can identify different food and drinks and say what I like / don't like. **A2**

I like cheese.

1 _____
2 _____
3 _____
4 _____
5 _____

Got it? ____ / 5

5 I can order food and drink at a restaurant. **A2**

I'd like a sandwich, please.

1 _____
2 _____
3 _____
4 _____
5 _____

Got it? ____ / 5

6 I can ask questions and talk about eating habits. **A2**

I eat meat twice a week.

1 _____
2 _____
3 _____
4 _____
5 _____

Got it? ____ / 5

Reading, listening, and writing

		Got It?		
		Yes	I'm not sure	No
7	I can understand a text about a skateboarder. **A2**	☐	☐	☐
8	I can write an e-mail about a future trip. **A2**	☐	☐	☐
9	I can understand a text about a famous chef. **A2**	☐	☐	☐
10	I can write about my diet. **A2**	☐	☐	☐

1 🔘 **Read and listen** What subject are Zoe and Sam studying?

a math   b history   c geography

Zoe   Right, Sam, geography. The Mississippi is longer than the Sacramento River. True or false?

Sam   I don't know. False?

Zoe   No, Sam, it's longer. Let's try again. The Appalachian Mountains are higher than the Rockies. True or false?

Sam   That's true.

Zoe   No, it's false, Sam. The Rockies are higher. You're hopeless!

Sam   Ask me about cities. They're more interesting than boring mountains.

Zoe   OK. Is New York bigger or smaller than Los Angeles?

Sam   Easy! New York is bigger.

Zoe   That's better! Here's a harder question. What's the population of New York City?

Sam   It's 8.3 million.

Zoe   Yes, I'm impressed! What's the population of Los Angeles?

Sam   It's about 4 million!

Zoe   Correct! You're almost as smart as me!

Sam   OK then, smart aleck. Why don't I ask you a question?

Zoe   OK. Fire away!

Sam   Why is the Mississippi a strange river?

Zoe   I don't know! Why?

Sam   Because it has four "i"s but it can't see.

Check it out!

| smart aleck | Fire away! |

2 Comprehension Complete the sentences with words in the box.

the Appalachians   Los Angeles
Los Angeles   Mississippi   New York
New York   the Rockies   Sacramento

1 The _____ is longer than the _____ River.

2 _____ are higher than _____.

3 _____ is bigger than _____.

4 _____ has 8.3 million inhabitants.

5 _____ has 4 million inhabitants.

Language focus

3 Dialogue focus Write the sentences in the correct order.

1 Zoe The Mississippi (longer / is / than) the Sacramento River. True or false?

The Mississippi is longer than the Sacramento River. True or false?

Sam I don't know. False?

2 Zoe The Appalachian Mountains (than / are / higher) the Rockies. True or false?

1 _____

Sam That's true.

3 Sam Ask me about cities. They're (than / interesting / more) boring mountains.

2 _____

Zoe OK. Is New York (or / smaller / than / bigger) Los Angeles?

3 _____

Sam Easy! New York is bigger.

Zoe Correct! You're almost (as / as / smart) me! 4 _____

4 💿 **Listen and check. Then listen and repeat.**

5 Focus on you Write sentences comparing the U.S. and Japan. Use the information in the chart and the phrases in the box.

are higher than   is bigger than   is longer than

	the U.S.	Japan	Brazil
rivers	the Mississippi	the Shinano	the Amazon
	(3,733 km)	(367 km)	(6,575 km)
mountains	Mount McKinley	Mount Fuji	Neblina Peak
	(6,194 m)	(3,776 m)	(3,014 m)
cities	New York City	Tokyo	São Paulo
	(8.3 million)	(12.8 million)	(11 million)

The Mississippi is longer than the Shinano.

6 Pairwork **Now compare Brazil with the U.S.**

The Amazon is longer than the Mississippi.

Geography

1 **Match the geographical features in column A with the names in column B.**

A	B
1 mountain	a Barbados
2 river	b the Sahara
3 lake	c Asia
4 island	d the Nile
5 continent	e the Mediterranean
6 country	f Lake Superior
7 desert	g the Atlantic
8 volcano	h Mount Vesuvius
9 sea	i Mount Everest
10 ocean	j Canada

2 **Listen and check. Then listen and repeat.**

3 **Look at the map and use the words in the box to complete the description of Hawaii.**

> islands   lake   mountain   ~~Ocean~~   river   sea   volcanoes

Hawaii is a U.S. state situated in the center of the Pacific _Ocean_, south west of the United States. The Big Island of Hawaii is one of a chain of eight ¹_____. Big Island is a volcanic island and there are five ²_____: Kohala, Mauna Kea, Hualâlai, Mauna Loa, and Kílauea. Mauna Loa and Kílauea are still active. The high ³_____ areas are in the north and the center of the island. Mauna Kea is 4,205 m above ⁴_____ level. There is a small ⁵_____ near the top of the mountain. Its name is Lake Waiau. Hawaii only has one ⁶_____, the Wailuku. It is 42 km long.

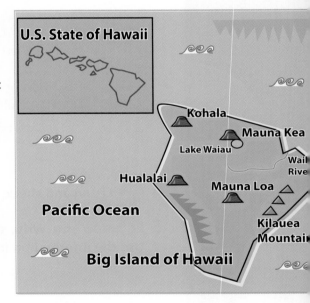

U.S. State of Hawaii

Kohala
Mauna Kea
Lake Waiau
Hualalai
Mauna Loa
Wail Rive
Kilauea Mountai
Pacific Ocean
Big Island of Hawaii

4 **Pairwork** **Complete the factfile about South America. Add two more names for each category.**

South America

- Important rivers: _the Amazon, the Paraná, ..._
- Important mountains: _Aconcagua, Ojos del Salado, ..._
- Important lakes: _Lake Maracaibo, Lake Titicaca, ..._
- Important islands:
  Grande de Tierra del Fuego, the Galápagos, ...
- Important seas / oceans: _the Caribbean Sea, ..._
- Important cities: _São Paulo, Bogotá, ..._

Comparative adjectives
Short adjectives

Adjective		Comparative
tall	+ -er	taller (than)
nice	+ -r	nicer (than)
hot	double the consonant + -er	hotter (than)
happy	- ~~y~~ + -ier	happier (than)

Rules p.W38

1 Write sentences with the comparative form of the adjectives.

Mumbai (population: 14 million)
Bangkok (population: 7 million) (big)
Mumbai is bigger than Bangkok.

1 The Yangtze River (6,300 km)
The Nile (6,695 km) (long)
2 Mount K2 (8,611 m)
Mount Everest (8,850 m) (high)
3 The Pacific Ocean (4,300m)
The Atlantic Ocean (3,600m) (deep)
4 The Empire State Building (381 m)
Willis Tower (442 m) (tall)
5 Alaska (average winter temperature -20°C / -30°C)
Hawaii (average winter temperature 25°C) (hot)

2 Write sentences comparing Luiza and Marcella with the adjectives in the box.

Luiza is taller than Marcella.

happy	old
pretty	~~tall~~
short	slim
young	

Luiza

Marcella

Long adjectives

Adjective		Comparative
important	more + adjective	more important (than)
boring		more boring (than)
interesting		more interesting (than)

Rules p.W38

3 Write sentences with the comparative form of the adjectives.

geography / history (interesting)
Geography is more interesting than history.

1 skateboarding / skiing (exciting)
2 trains / airplanes (slow)
3 chimpanzees / dogs (intelligent)
4 the library / the gym (quiet)
5 cell phones / MP3 players (expensive)
6 Angelina Jolie / Julianne Moore (famous)
7 cars / motorcycles (safe)
8 cats / dogs (independent)

Irregular adjectives

Adjective	Comparative
good	**better** (than)
bad	**worse** (than)
far	**further** (than)

Rules p.W38

4 Complete the sentences with the comparative form of the adjectives.

I think that reality shows are <u>better</u> (good) than quiz shows.

1 Last week's science test was bad, but this week's test was _____ (bad)!
2 Which city is _____ (pretty) – Paris or Venice?
3 Boston is _____ (far) from New York than Philadelphia.
4 English is _____ (easy) than Chinese.
5 Summer in Australia is _____ (hot) than summer in the U.K.
6 Fantasy movies are _____ (interesting) than animated movies.
7 Small towns are _____ (safe) than big cities.

Finished?

Make a list of two singers, two TV hosts, and two actors.

Write sentences with the comparative form of the adjectives in the box.

| bad | boring | funny | good |
| intelligent | interesting | ~~old~~ | talented |

Fergie is older than Rihanna.

Asking for tourist information

1 🔘 **Listen and complete the dialogue with the questions in the box. Listen and check. Then listen and repeat.**

> ~~Can I help you~~   How can I get there   How much are the tickets
> What time does it open   Where is it

Assistant	Good morning. _Can I help you?_
Paula	Yes, please. I want to visit the Empire State Building. ¹_____?
Assistant	They're $20 for adults and $14 for children.
Paula	²_____?
Assistant	It's open from 8 a.m. to 2 a.m. every day. There aren't as many people there at 1 p.m. as at 11 p.m.
Paula	³_____?
Assistant	It's on 5th Avenue. Between 33rd and 34th Streets.
Paula	⁴_____?
Assistant	You can take the subway to 34th Street or get a bus. The bus is as fast as the subway and you can see the city. Or you can walk. It takes about 45 minutes and it's less expensive than the bus or the subway!
Paula	Thanks.
Assistant	You're welcome. Have a nice day!

You ask	You answer
How much are the tickets?	They're $20. / The tickets cost …
What time does it open / close / start / finish?	It opens / starts at … It closes / finishes at …
Where is it?	It's on / near / in …
How can I get there?	You can take the subway / take a bus / walk.

2 🔘 **Pronunciation /ə/ Listen and repeat.**

You can see the city.   How much are the tickets?   It's cheaper than the bus.

3 🔘 **Listen and circle the schwa sound /ə/ in the words below.**

1 ex(e)rcise   2 open   3 children   4 welcome   5 Saturday   6 eleven

4 🔘 **Listen and complete the information in the factfile. Then listen and check.**

THE GUGGENHEIM MUSEUM	Adult ticket: ¹_____ Closes at: ⁴_____ Child ticket: ²_____ Transportation: ⁵_____ Opens at: ³_____

5 Pairwork Use the factfile to write a dialogue. 🎭

> **Madame Tussauds**
> NEW YORK ✈
>
> **Adult ticket:** $35.00
> **Child ticket:** $28.00
> **Opening times:** 10 a.m. – 6 p.m.
> **Location:** West 42nd Street (between 7th / 8th Avenues)
> **Transportation:** subway to 42nd Street / Times Square or bus

Grammar

as ... as

The *Harry Potter* movies aren't	as	good	as	the books.
Manaus isn't	as	big	as	Rio de Janeiro.
Are Linkin Park	as	popular	as	U2?

Rules p.W39

1 Write sentences with *as ... as* and the adjectives in the box.

> big ~~cheap~~ cold expensive
> good heavy ~~old~~ tall

I'm 13 years old. My friend is 13 years old.
I'm _as old as my friend._
The red T-shirt is $12. The blue T-shirt is $10.
The red T-shirt _isn't as cheap as the blue T-shirt._

1 Hong Kong (7 million people). Dhaka (7 million people)
Dhaka _____.
2 Elephants weigh about 5,000 kg. Giraffes weigh about 1,300 kg.
Giraffes _____.
3 It's -6°C in Moscow. It's -6°C in Chicago.
Moscow _____.
4 Koji got a B in his test. Emi got an A in her test.
Koji's test _____.
5 Lucas is 1m 68cm. Mili is 1m 68cm.
Mili _____.
6 A burger is $4. A pizza is $6.
A burger _____.

2 Rewrite the sentences using *as ... as.*

Skiing is more difficult than swimming.
Swimming isn't as difficult as skiing.

1 Reality shows are worse than talent shows.
_____
2 Will Smith is funnier than Jim Carrey.
_____
3 History is more interesting than math.
_____
4 The climate in Hawaii is hotter than the climate in Chile.
_____
5 Taking the bus is cheaper than taking the subway.
_____
6 Cats are cleaner than dogs.
_____

less ... than

A Fiat car is	less	expensive	than	a Ferrari.
Dogs are	less	intelligent	than	monkeys.

Rules p.W39

3 Write sentences giving your opinion. Use *less ... than.*

Daniel Radcliffe / Robert Patterson (talented)
Daniel Radcliffe is less talented than Robert Patterson. or
Robert Patterson is less talented than Daniel Radcliffe.

1 trains / buses (expensive)
_____
2 MP3 players / cell phones (useful)
_____
3 Jay-Z / Daddy Yankee (famous)
_____
4 action movies / horror movies (exciting)
_____
5 Kirsten Stewart / Emma Watson (attractive)
_____
6 New York / Sydney (populated)
_____
7 geography / science (interesting)
_____

4 Game! Think of two words for each category. Then ask your partner to say a comparative sentence about each of them. Give your partner one point for each correct sentence.

> cities countries drink food
> jobs movies music
> sports transportation

A Countries: The U.S. and Japan.
B The U.S. is bigger than Japan. (✓ = 1 point)
The U.S. is more big than Japan. (✗ = 0 points)

> Finished?

Write your opinions about the places and things in exercise 4.

Bizarre pets!

Do you have a pet? Is it a cat, a dog, or is it a snake? Cats and dogs are traditional pets, but more and more people are getting unusual pets. What are the pros and cons? Let's find out.

Corn snakes

Snakes are becoming popular pets, especially corn snakes. They come from the south-eastern and central parts of the U.S. and Mexico. Corn snakes aren't as dangerous as other snakes and they're easier to keep.

They're good pets because …

- they're smaller and cheaper than other snakes
- they aren't poisonous and they aren't aggressive
- they have beautiful colors and patterns

They're bad pets because …

- they're very timid
- they're nocturnal so they sleep all day and are active at night
- the temperature in your house has to be between 21°C and 23°C because they come from warm countries
- their favorite food is mice

Tarantulas

Tarantulas live in warm countries all over the world. Their name comes from the town of Taranto in Italy. In the past, the people there called large spiders tarantola. When Italian explorers went to South America in the 16th century they used the same name for the big spiders they found.

They're good pets because …

- they don't need much space and they're easier to keep than other exotic animals
- they have a simple diet of insects
- they are very clean and they don't carry diseases

They're bad pets because …

- they're poisonous and they bite (but a tarantula bite is less serious than people think)

Reading

1 Read the text. Then answer the questions.

Where do corn snakes come from? *Corn snakes come from the south-eastern and central parts of the U.S. and Mexico.*

1 When are they active?
2 What do they eat?
3 How expensive are they, compared to other snakes?
4 Where does the name tarantula come from?
5 What do tarantulas eat?
6 Why are they sometimes bad pets?
7 How serious is a tarantula bite?

Listening

2 🔘 **Listen to a pet shop owner advising a boy about guinea pigs and hamsters. Are the sentences are true or false?**

Guinea pigs and hamsters are rodents. _True_
They belong to the same family as dogs and foxes. _False_
1 Guinea pigs are from South Africa. _____
2 Hamsters are bigger than guinea pigs. _____
3 Hamsters are usually 10 cm long. _____
4 Guinea pigs usually live two to three years. _____
5 Guinea pigs like company. _____
6 Hamsters sometimes bite. _____
7 Hamsters are more aggressive than guinea pigs. _____
8 Guinea pigs are less expensive than hamsters. _____

guinea pig

3 🔘 **Listen again and correct the false sentences.**

They belong to the same family as dogs and foxes. False.
They belong to the same family as rabbits and rats.

hamster

Speaking

4 Pairwork Choose your favorite animals from box A. Tell your partner and compare them with the adjectives in box B. 🎭

A
| cat chimpanzee dog dolphin horse |
| iguana kangaroo rabbit snake tiger |

B
| aggressive beautiful boring clean cool expensive |
| friendly independent intelligent interesting |

A My favorite animals are dolphins.
B Really? My favorite animals are horses.
A Dolphins are more intelligent than horses.
B But horses are friendlier than dolphins.
A That isn't true. Dolphins are as friendly as horses. Horses are sometimes aggressive and they can bite.
B You can't have a pet dolphin.
A That's true. But horses are very expensive.

Writing

5 Imagine you want to buy a pet, but you can't decide between a traditional pet and an exotic pet. Write a short paragraph and answer the questions about each animal.

I want to buy a pet, but I can't decide between a ... and a ....
● What do they look like?
● How big are they?
● How much do they cost?
● Are they aggressive / friendly?
● What do they eat?
● Do they need a lot of space?

8 The best day of my life!

Check it out!

Guess what! You bet!
Way to go!

1 💿 **Read and listen What is Sam's report card like?**

> **a** very good   **b** OK   **c** very bad

Zoe   Did you get your report card today, Sam?
Sam   Yes, I did, but I don't want to open it.
I'm very worried. The exams were so difficult.
Teo   Which exam was the worst?
Sam   Math was definitely the most difficult.
I was really nervous. But, thanks to Zoe, geography was the easiest.

At Sam's house …

Sam   Hi, Mom, here's my report card.
You open it.
Mom   Oh, Sam!
Sam   What?
Mom   These are your best results ever!
Sam   Seriously?

Mom   Yes! Good job! Here's your cell phone.
Call Coach Carson and tell him.
Sam   Thanks, Mom! Oh, I'm so excited!

On the phone …

CC   Hello.
Sam   Hello, Coach, it's Sam! Guess what! I passed my exams!
CC   Way to go, Sam! The final is on Saturday! Are you ready to play?
Sam   You bet! This is the best day of my life!

2 Comprehension Answer the questions.

What did Sam think about the exams?
Sam thought the exams were very difficult.
1 Which exam was the worst?
2 Which exam was the easiest?
3 What's happening on Saturday?

Language focus

3 Dialogue focus Complete the dialogues with the phrases in the box.

the best   the easiest   the most difficult   the worst   your best

1 Teo Which exam was <u>the worst</u>?

Sam Math was definitely
1 _____.
I was really nervous.
But, thanks to Zoe,
geography was
2 _____.

2 Mom Oh, Sam!
Sam What?
Mom These are
3 _____
results ever!
Sam Seriously?

3 CC Way to go, Sam! The
final is on Saturday!
Are you ready to play?
Sam You bet! This is
4 _____
day of my life!

4 🔘 **Listen and check. Then listen and repeat.**

5 Focus on you Write dialogues to ask for and give opinions about the things in the box.

city in the U.S.   day of the week   month of the year
show on TV   pop song of the year

A What's the best show on TV?
B It's *Good Luck Charlie*.
A I agree. I think it's fantastic, too. / Really? I think it's terrible.

6 Pairwork Practice the dialogues in exercise 5.

Vocabulary

Feelings and emotions

1 Look at the pictures. Read and listen to the adjectives. Then listen and repeat.

1 happy

2 nervous

3 proud

4 sad

5 frightened

6 bored

7 embarrassed

8 excited

9 confident

10 angry

11 annoyed

12 fed up

2 Copy the adjectives from exercise 1 into the correct columns.

Positive adjectives	Negative adjectives
happy	nervous
_____	_____
_____	_____

3 Choose the correct answers.

Luke did very well in his exam. We're very **happy** / **proud** of him!

1 I'm really **angry** / **excited**! I told Jenny a secret and she told everyone!
2 Chloe won first prize. Her parents are very **proud** / **confident**.
3 Mark's mom showed me his baby photos! He was really **frightened** / **embarrassed**!
4 Hannah's **sad** / **excited** because her best friend can't come to her birthday party.
5 It's raining and Jack can't play soccer. He's **fed up** / **nervous**.

4 **Pairwork** Ask and answer questions about your emotions.

it's the last day of high school   it's your birthday   you get a good grade
you receive a present   you watch a horror movie
your brother / sister takes your CDs   your teacher gives you extra homework

A How do you feel when you receive a present?
B I usually feel happy.

CD-ROM ▶ **Workbook p. W46**

Grammar

Superlative adjectives
Short adjectives

Adjective		Superlative	
tall		+ -est	the tall**est**
nice		+ -st	the nice**st**
hot	*the* + adjective	double the consonant	the sad**dest**
happy		-y + -iest	the happ**iest**

Rules p.W44

1 Write the superlative form of these adjectives.

small <u>the smallest</u>

1 large _____
2 old _____
3 hot _____
4 noisy _____
5 new _____
6 crazy _____
7 close _____
8 red _____
9 busy _____

2 Write sentences with the superlative form of the adjectives.

Mrs. Thompson / nice / teacher in my school
<u>Mrs. Thompson is the nicest teacher in my school.</u>

1 the living room / big / room in the house
_____

2 Uncle Richard / funny / person in my family
_____

3 fall / pretty / season of the year
_____

4 Mark / tall / boy in the class
_____

5 today / happy / day of my life
_____

Long adjectives

Adjective		Superlative
boring		the most boring
important	*the most* + adjective	the most important
interesting		the most interesting

Rules p.W44

3 Complete the sentences with the superlative form of the adjectives.

Luke is <u>the most popular</u> boy in the class. (popular)

1 I think that San Francisco is _____ city in the U.S. (beautiful)
2 Japanese is _____ language to learn. (difficult)
3 The crocodile is one of _____ animals in Australia. (dangerous)
4 I think snowboarding is _____ winter sport. (exciting)
5 Yao Ming is _____ person in China. (famous)
6 Moscow is one of _____ cities in the world. (expensive)

4 Complete the sentences with the superlative forms of the adjectives in the box.

cold	expensive	fast	heavy
	populated	~~tall~~	

The *Burj Khalifa* building in Dubai is <u>the tallest</u> building in the world. It's 818 meters tall.

1 The Bugatti Veyron is _____ car in the world. It costs $1.7 million!
2 African elephants are _____ land animals in the world. They can weigh up to 6,000 kg!
3 Tokyo is _____ city in the world. About 35 million people live in or around the city!
4 Birds are _____ animals in the world. Peregrine falcons can fly 170 km/h!
5 Antarctica is _____ place in the world. It can be -90°C in winter!

Finished?

Write sentences about the students in your class and the subjects you study. Use the superlative form of the adjectives in the box.

difficult	easy	old	tall	young

Sergio is the tallest person in my class.
Math is the most difficult subject.

CD-ROM **Workbook pp. W46–W47**

Making a phone call

1 🔘 **Listen to and read the dialogues. Then answer the questions. Listen and check. Then listen and repeat.**

1

A Hello.

B Hi! It's Becky. Is this Meg?

A No, it isn't. It's her sister. Meg isn't here at the moment. She's at her dance class. Do you want to leave a message?

B Yes, please. Can you ask her to return my call before 8 o'clock at the latest? My number is 212-555-0911.

A That's 212-555-0911. OK. Bye.

B Bye.

2

A Hello.

B Hello. Can I speak with Rick, please?

A Yes, certainly. Who's calling?

B It's Harry, Rick's best friend.

A Oh, hi Harry! Hang on a minute. Rick! It's for you. It's Harry.

	Phone call 1	Phone call 2
Who is making the phone call?		
Who does he / she want to speak with?		
Is he / she successful?		

You ask	You answer
Can I speak with ...?	Yes, certainly. Sorry, (*Meg / Harry*) isn't here right now.
Who's calling? / Is that ...?	It's (*Meg / Harry*). / Yes, it is. / No, it isn't.
Do you want to leave a message?	Yes, please. Can you tell him / her ...? / Can you ask him / her to return my call? No, thanks.

2 🔘 **Pronunciation** /h/ **Listen and repeat.**

A Who's calling?

B It's Harry.

A Hi, Harry! Hang on a minute.

3 🔘 **Listen and check (✓) the words you hear.**

1 hand ☐   and ☐

2 his ☐   is ☐

3 at ☐   hat ☐

4 high ☐   I ☐

5 ate ☐   hate ☐

4 **Pairwork** **Read the instructions below and prepare a short dialogue.**

A Answer the phone.

B Ask to speak with your friend (give name).

A Say he / she isn't at home and ask who it is.

B Say who you are.

A Ask if B wants to leave a message.

B Say yes and ask A to tell your friend to return your call.

Grammar

Superlative adjectives
Irregular adjectives

Adjective	Superlative
good	the best
bad	the worst
far	the furthest

Rules p.W45

1 Complete the sentences with the superlative form of the adjectives.

Friday is <u>the best</u> day of the week. (good)

1 This song is _____ song on the CD. (bad)
2 Which is _____ pizzeria in your city? (busy)
3 Which American city is _____ from New York? (far)
4 The Air and Space Museum is one of _____ museums in Arizona. (interesting)
5 Mrs. Santos is _____ teacher. (good)

Comparative / Superlative

Think!

Read the sentences. Then choose the correct option.

The Amazon is longer than the Yangtze.
The Nile is the longest river in the world.

- We use the [1]comparative / superlative to compare two people or things.
- We use the [2]comparative / superlative to compare more than two people or things.

Rules p.W45

2 Write sentences with the comparative and superlative forms of the adjectives.

Louise (11) / Emma (14) / Serena (15) (old)
Emma is older than Louise. Serena is the oldest.

1 Venezuela (912,050 km^2) / Ecuador (283,560 km^2) / Peru (1,285,220 km^2) (big)
2 A Fiat (€19,170) / A Volkswagen (€34,906) / A Ferrari (€229,150) (expensive)
3 Mont Blanc (4,810m) / Aconcagua (6,962 m) / Mount Everest (8,850 m) (high)
4 Tom (1.68 m) / Caroline (1.62 m) / Joshua (1.57 m) (tall)
5 London (18°C) / Athens (34°C) / Boston (26°C) (hot)

the least

Adjective	Superlative
boring	the least boring
important	the least important
interesting	the least interesting

Rules p.W45

3 Rewrite the sentences with *the least* and one of the adjectives in the box.

confident   dangerous   difficult
~~expensive~~   interesting   noisy

Buses are the cheapest form of public transportation in the U.S.
Buses are the <u>least expensive</u> form of public transportation in the U.S.

1 Jack is the most nervous boy in the class.
Jack is _____ boy in the class.
2 He is the most boring host on TV.
He is _____ host on TV.
3 History is the easiest subject at school.
History is _____ subject at school.
4 The library is the quietest place in the school.
The library is _____ place in the school.
5 This is the safest area in the city.
This is _____ area in the city.

4 Game! Complete the sentences with the comparative or the superlative form of the adjectives in parentheses. Are the sentences true or false?

A kilometer is <u>longer than</u> a mile. (long)	T	Ⓕ
1 São Paulo is _____ New York. (big)	T	F
2 Uruguay is _____ country in South America. (small)	T	F
3 The Pacific Ocean is _____ ocean in the world. (deep)	T	F
4 Bill Gates is _____ man in the U.S. (rich)	T	F
5 A Ferrari is _____ a Rolls-Royce. (expensive)	T	F
6 A giraffe is _____ an elephant. (fast)	T	F

Finished?

Write three more sentences for the quiz. Ask your classmates if they are true or false.

Seoul is the biggest city in South Korea.

CD-ROM   Workbook pp. W46–W47

COLOR
your emotions

American people sometimes say that they "feel blue" when they are sad and they "see red" when they are angry. How do colors affect our emotions?

1 Colors affect our emotions because they influence chemicals in our bodies. These chemicals are called hormones. Hormones control our feelings.

2 Some colors, for example blue and green, are relaxing. Green is the most relaxing color. It is the best color for your bedroom. It can also help you feel calm when you are worried or nervous. That is why doctors and nurses often wear green uniforms in hospitals.

3 Red, orange, and yellow are positive colors. We feel happy and excited when we see them. They're the best colors to wear when you are fed up or sad. Yellow is also good when you have an exam at school. It helps you feel confident and improves your memory. But these colors can also be negative. People can become impatient, irritable, and angry when they see them.

4 Our culture also influences our relationship with color. In China, for example, people wear white to funerals. But in Western culture, black is the color of death and white symbolizes peace and purity. Western brides often wear white, but Chinese brides wear red. In China, red symbolizes happiness and fortune.

Reading

1 Read the text and then match each heading to a paragraph.

- Cultural influences
- Positive, exciting colors
- Relaxing colors
- Colors and our emotions

2 Answer the questions.

Why do colors affect our emotions?
Because they influence chemicals in our bodies.

1 What colors help us feel calm and relaxed?
2 Why are red, orange, and yellow positive colors?
3 Why can they be negative, too?
4 When do Chinese people wear white clothes?
5 What does red symbolize in China?

Listening

3 Listen to two teenagers talking about their favorite colors and how colors affect their emotions. Choose the correct answers.

David

He **likes** / **doesn't like** strong colors.

1 David's favorite color is **light blue / black**.
2 He feels **sad and boring** / **happy and confident** when he wears his black and red jacket.
3 His bedroom walls are **light green / white**.

Sonia

4 Sonia **loves / hates** the color black.
5 Her favorite color is **red / orange**.
6 She usually feels **sad / happy** when she wears her winter coat.
7 Her bedroom walls are **orange / light green**.

Speaking

4 Pairwork Ask and answer questions about your favorite colors.

- What is your favorite color?
- How do you feel when you see it?
- What color do you like wearing?
- How do you feel when you are wearing it?
- What color is your bedroom?
- What color don't you like?

5 Tell the class about your partner's favorite colors and how he / she feels about them.

Writing

6 Write a text about your favorite colors and how you feel about them. Use the questions in exercise 4 to help you.

Vocabulary

1 **Write the names of the numbered items in the picture.**

> ~~continent~~   country   island   lake
> mountain   ocean   river   sea   volcano

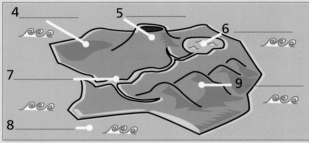

2 **Complete the sentences with an adjective of feeling or emotion.**

1 Don't be f_____! It's a big dog, but it's friendly.
2 Mom's very a_____! The cat ate our goldfish!
3 I'm f_____ u_____! It's Sunday and there's school tomorrow.
4 We're very p_____ of Enrique. He won an art competition.
5 Monica's very h_____. Her boyfriend gave her some flowers.
6 The boys are e_____. Their soccer team is in the championship final.
7 Are you n_____ about the exam tomorrow?
8 Vera's cell phone rang at the movies. She was very e_____.

Grammar

3 **Complete the sentences with the comparative form of the adjectives.**

> Is Alaska larger (large) than Texas?

1 Do you think English is _____ (easy) than math?
2 It's quite cold today. Yesterday was _____ (warm).
3 Are the Black Eyed Peas _____ (good) than Green Day?
4 Their apartment is _____ (nice) than our apartment.
5 I think museums are _____ (interesting) than art galleries.
6 Elephants are _____ (heavy) than giraffes.
7 These exam results are _____ (bad) than your results last year.
8 Cleveland is a _____ (safe) city than Detroit.
9 Vanessa Hudgens is _____ (talented) than Ashley Tisdale.
10 Fortaleza is _____ (far) from Brasília than Recife.

4 **Write sentences comparing the computer and the TV with as ... as.**

TV
Price: $899.00
Size: 103 cm x 63 cm x 8 cm
Weight: 27 kg
Popularity rating: *****

Lap top
Price: $499.00
Size: 2.5 cm x 33 cm x 25 cm
Weight: 2.5 kg
Popularity rating: ***

> small The TV isn't as small as the computer.

1 expensive _____
2 big _____
3 heavy _____
4 popular _____

5 **Rewrite the sentences with less ... than.**

> Superman 2 was more exciting than Superman 3.
> Superman 3 was less exciting than "Superman 2".

1 Katy Perry isn't as famous as Justin Timberlake.
Katy Perry is _____.
2 Cars are usually more expensive than motorcycles.
Motorcycles are usually _____.
3 South Korea isn't as populated as Japan.
South Korea is _____.
4 The volcano Mount St. Helens is more active than Mount Rainier.
Mount Rainier is _____.

6 **Complete the questions with the superlative forms of the adjectives. Then write personal answers.**

Who is <u>the oldest</u> person in your family? (old)
My grandma is the oldest person in my family. She's 74 years old.

1 What is _____ subject for you at school? (easy)

2 Who is _____ person in history? (important)

3 What is _____ program on TV? (good)

4 Who is _____ person in your class? (nice)

5 What is _____ tourist attraction in your country? (popular)

6 What is _____ day of the week for you? (bad)

7 **Write sentences comparing the actors. Use the comparative, superlative, and *the least* forms of the adjectives in the box.**

beautiful   short   old   talented
~~tall~~   young

Name:	Keira Knightley
Birth date:	March 26th, 1985
Height:	170 cm

Name:	Ashley Tisdale
Birth date:	July 2nd, 1985
Height:	160 cm

Name:	Lucy Liu
Birth date:	December 2nd, 1968
Height:	157 cm

<u>Kiera Knightly is taller than Ashley Tisdale, but Lucy Liu is the least tall.</u>

1 _____

2 _____

3 _____

4 _____

5 _____

Got it?

8 **Read the text about Florida. Choose the correct answers.**

Florida is in the south-east of the U.S. Florida is one of (the most)/ most beautiful states in the U.S. with a lot of lakes, rivers, and beaches. Two [1]**better / of the best** beaches are Siesta Key Beach and Turtle Beach. Turtle Beach isn't [2]**as popular as / as popular than** Siesta Key, but it's [3]**more interesting / most interesting** because there are a lot of birds and animals. There are some really cool animals in Florida! Manatees, for example, are related to elephants but they're [4]**smaller /smallest** and they live in water! There are also about 200,000 alligators! They are [5]**less / the least** dangerous than people think because they are frightened of humans and are [6]**more active / most active** at night than in the day.

Today Florida is [7]**more / most** famous for its theme parks than for its animals. Disney World and Universal Studios are two of [8]**the more / the most** popular tourist attractions in the U.S!

9 **Answer the questions.**

1 Where is Florida?

_____

2 Why is Turtle Beach more interesting than Siesta Beach?

_____

3 What is the difference between manatees and elephants?

_____

4 Why are alligators less dangerous than people think?

_____

5 What are the most popular tourist attractions in the U.S?

_____

GUINNESS WORLD RECORDS

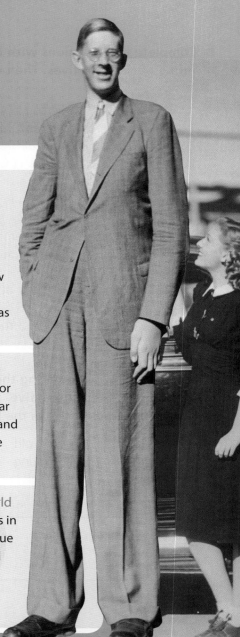

Guinness World Records is a famous book of world records about people, animals, and the natural world. It started in 1951 and there is a new edition every year. Today the book has its own world record. It's the best-selling non-religious book in the world!

• **The highest jump by a pig**
Kotetsu, a black pig from Japan is a world record holder, too. In August 2004, the pig jumped 70 cm! It's the world record for the highest jump by a pig!

• **The tallest person in history**
The tallest man in history was an American, Robert Wadlow. He was 2.72 m tall! Wadlow was born in Illinois in 1918. At first his height was normal, but he started to grow very quickly when he was four years old. At the age of eight he was already 1.88 m! He died in 1940.

• **The longest karaoke in the world**
A woman from South Korea sang for more than 76 hours in a karaoke bar in Seoul. She started on Thursday and sang about 1,200 songs before she finished on Saturday afternoon!

• **The biggest barbeque in the world**
More than 1,250 barbeque fanatics in Uruguay cooked beef on a barbeque that was 1.5 km long! They cooked 12,000 kg of beef for about 20,000 people! It was the world's biggest barbeque!

1 Answer the questions.

1 What is Guinness World Records?
2 What world record does the book have?
3 How high did Kotetsu the pig jump?
4 How tall was the tallest man in history?
5 How many songs did the karaoke champion sing?
6 Where was the world's biggest barbeque?

2 Focus on you Find out about a world record holder from your country. Look in the Guinness World Records book or on the website (www.guinessworldrecords.com). Write a short paragraph. Say:

• the name of the person
• his / her age
• where he / she is from
• the record he / she has

My progress

D

Speaking and writing

1 I can compare people, places, and things.   **A2**

<u>Brazil is the biggest country in South America.</u>

1 _____
2 _____
3 _____
4 _____
5 _____

Got it? ____ / 5

2 I can ask for information at a tourist center.   **A2**

<u>How much are the tickets?</u>

1 _____
2 _____
3 _____
4 _____
5 _____

Got it? ____ / 5

3 I can identify different feelings and emotions.   **A2**

<u>happy</u>

1 _____
2 _____
3 _____
4 _____
5 _____

Got it? ____ / 5

4 I can ask and answer questions about how I feel in different situations.   **A2**

<u>I feel excited on my birthday.</u>

1 _____
2 _____
3 _____
4 _____
5 _____

Got it? ____ / 5

5 I can ask and answer questions on the phone.   **A2**

<u>Can I speak with Martha?</u>

1 _____
2 _____
3 _____
4 _____
5 _____

Got it? ____ / 5

6 I can ask and answer questions about my favorite colors.   **A2**

<u>I like wearing red clothes.</u>

1 _____
2 _____
3 _____
4 _____
5 _____

Got it? ____ / 5

Reading, listening, and writing

		Got It?	
	Yes	I'm not sure	No
7 I can identify geographical features and complete a fact file about South America. **A2**	☐	☐	☐
8 I can read and understand a text about strange pets. **A2**	☐	☐	☐
9 I can write about my favorite animals and pets. **A2**	☐	☐	☐
10 I can understand a text about how colors affect emotions. **A2**	☐	☐	☐

What is an orchestra?

The word *orchestra* comes from Ancient Greek. In Ancient Greek, *orchestra* describes the area in front of a stage. Today the meaning is different and it describes a large
5 group of musicians. An orchestra sits in a special area below the stage when there are actors, singers, or dancers, but when an orchestra performs on their own, they sit on the stage.

10 An orchestra plays pieces of music together on different instruments. Orchestras usually play classical music, but sometimes they play pop music and music for movies.

There are two kinds of orchestra: a symphony
15 orchestra and a chamber orchestra. The word *symphony* comes from two Greek words: *sym* means "together" and *phonos* means "sound". Classical symphony orchestras are big. They usually have about one hundred
20 musicians and between eighteen and twenty-five different instruments. Chamber orchestras usually have about fifty musicians.

In a symphony orchestra, there are four different groups of instruments: strings,
25 brass, woodwind, and percussion. There are different numbers of instruments in each group. There are usually between sixty and seventy string instruments, for example violins and harps. In the brass section, there
30 are usually fifteen instruments and there are between two and five trumpets. There are about sixteen woodwind instruments, for example flutes and clarinets. There are lots of percussion instruments, but there are usually
35 only four musicians, or percussionists, in this section.

Each group of instruments in an orchestra has a special place. First, there is the string section, then the woodwind section, then the
40 brass section, and finally the percussion section is at the back. The conductor stands in front of all the musicians.

The conductor's job is very difficult. The conductor tells the orchestra when and how
45 to play. The conductor uses a baton to direct the orchestra. Each musician only knows the music for their instrument. The conductor knows the music for all the instruments.

Useful language

strings (n) *line 24*
brass (n) *line 25*
woodwind (n) *line 25*
percussion (n) *line 25*
baton *line 45*

1 Read the text. Label the parts of the orchestra.

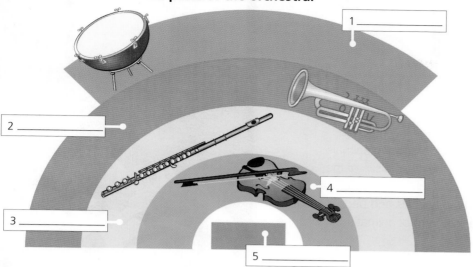

1 _____

2 _____

3 _____

4 _____

5 _____

2 Read the text again. Correct the mistake in each sentence.

The word *orchestra* comes from Ancient Egyptian.

The word "orchestra" comes from Ancient Greek.

1 Orchestras only play classical music.

_____

2 There are seventy musicians in a chamber orchestra.

_____

3 There are six different groups of instruments in a symphony orchestra.

_____

4 Violins and harps are in the percussion section.

_____

5 The conductor stands between the musicians.

_____

6 The conductor knows the music for one instrument.

_____

3 Answer the questions.

How many musicians are there in a symphony orchestra?

There are about 100 musicians.

1 What does the word *symphony* mean?

_____

2 How many groups of instruments are there in a symphony orchestra?

_____

3 How many string instruments are there in a symphony orchestra?

_____

4 How many trumpets are there usually in the brass section?

_____

5 What does a conductor use to conduct an orchestra?

_____

Project

Who is your favorite singer or band? Write a magazine review about one of their concerts. Think about …

- where the concert was
- what the concert was like
- the instruments
- the number of musicians

The world of animation

In the beginning

1 In the 1880s, Eadweard Muybridge invented the zoopraxiscope. He took photos of moving animals and people and put them on the glass disks of the zoopraxiscope. When the disks turned they projected the
5 images onto a screen and the animals and people seemed to move. This was the earliest form of animation. It was the first movie projector.

In 1895, Auguste and Louis Lumière invented the cinematograph, the world's first movie camera. Movie-
10 makers used the camera to produce stop-frame animation. They filmed something and then stopped the camera. They moved the object and then filmed it again.

Animated movies

The first animated movies appeared in the 1920s. Artists drew cartoon pictures on paper for every part of a movie.
15 The artists then put their drawings onto thin pieces of plastic, called cels. A photographer then took photos of each cel. Walt Disney made the first animated cartoon with sound in 1928, *Steamboat Willie*.

In 1937, the Disney Studios made *Snow White*. It was the
20 first animated movie with sound. It took three years and 300 artists to make *Snow White*.

CGI (computer-generated images)

In the 1960s, movie-makers began to experiment with computer technology and models for special effects. The models are three-dimensional and a computer program
25 controls their movements. Disney and a company called Pixar produced *Toy Story* in 1995. This was the first computer-generated movie. Twenty-seven animators worked on the movie and there were 400 different computer models. In total, there were 114,240 frames of animation
30 in the movie. Some of the complicated scenes took up to thirty hours to make!

Producers used modern movie techniques to remake the fantasy movie, *King Kong*. There was a 1933 version of the movie and it used stop-frame animation. The 2005 version
35 of the movie used CGI to create the special effects. Which one do you think was better?

Useful language

glass disks (n) *line 3*
animation (n) *line 6*
object (n) *line 12*
plastic (n) *line 16*
cel (n) *line 16*
movement (n) *line 25*

1 **Read the text. Match the types of animation in the box with the dates.**

animated cartoon   cartoon movie   CGI   cinematograph
first CGI movie   ~~zoopraxiscope~~

zoopraxiscope

| 1880s | 1895 | 1928 | 1937 | 1960s | 1995 |

2 **Read the text again. Are the sentences true or false? Correct the false sentences.**

Eadweard Muybridge invented the first movie projector. <u>True.</u>

1 The cinematograph produced the earliest form of animation.

_____

2 Auguste and Louis Lumière invented stop-frame animation.

_____

3 Walt Disney's work on animated movies began in the 1920s.

_____

4 *Snow White* was the first animated movie with sound.

_____

5 A complicated scene in *Toy Story* took less than twenty hours to make.

_____

3 **Answer the questions.**

How did stop-frame animation work?
<u>Movie-makers took a photo of an object, stopped the camera, moved the</u>
<u>object, and took another photo.</u>

1 What did artists use to produce animated pictures?

_____

2 Why was *Snow White* important in the history of animation?

_____

3 How long did it take to make *Snow White*?

_____

4 Why was *Toy Story* special?

_____

5 How many animators worked on *Toy Story*?

_____

6 What was the difference between the 1933 version and the 2005 version of *King Kong*?

_____

Project

Write a review about your favorite movie. Think about …

• the type of movie
• the type of animation
• the story
• the characters

FAIRTRADE

Look for the FAIRTRADE Mark on Fairtrade products.

1 Where does your food come from?

1 Do you know where your food comes from? Does it come from your own country? Does it travel by airplane? Do you buy your food at a supermarket, a local market, or from a farm?

2 _____

Farmers don't often receive a lot of money for their crops
5 because big international companies often take the profits from the food instead. But this started to change twenty-six years ago when a group of people had an idea. They wanted to help the farmers and Fairtrade began.

3 _____

With Fairtrade, farmers form co-operatives. A co-operative is a
10 business organization. It belongs to the members and they all want the same thing: to work together for everyone. The farmers produce their food and a co-operative buys the food.

4 _____

Fairtrade means that farmers in developing countries can earn more money for their crops. Farmers and their families can
15 escape poverty and have a better future. Fairtrade guarantees farmers a fair price for their crops and an extra amount of money to invest in their communities.

5 _____

There are many Fairtrade products now, from chocolate to bananas, tea, coffee, and even soccer balls! Bananas are one
20 of world's most popular fruits and a lot of bananas come from the Caribbean and Central and South America. 30,000 boxes a week travel from El Guabo in Ecuador to Europe and the U.S. Now the farmers in El Guabo receive a good price for their bananas thanks to Fairtrade.

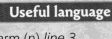

Useful language
farm (n) *line 3*
profit (n) *line 5*
business organization (n) *line 10*
produce (v) *line 12*
crop (n) *line 14*

1 Read the text quickly. How many Fairtrade products does it mention?

2 Read the text again. Match the titles to the paragraphs.

A Fairtrade foods

B In the past

C What is Fairtrade?

D ~~Where does your food come from?~~

E Why Fairtrade?

3 Answer the questions.

When did Fairtrade begin?

Fairtrade began twenty-six years ago.

1 What happens to the profits from food without Fairtrade?

_____

2 What is a co-operative?

_____

3 Where do Fairtrade farmers work?

_____

4 How does Fairtrade help farmers?

_____

5 According to the text, what is one of the most popular fruits in the world?

_____

4 Look at the pictures of the life of a Fairtrade banana. Put the pictures in the correct order.

Project

What is your favorite food? Write the story of its journey to your plate. Think about ...

- where it comes from
- how it grows
- who produces the food
- whether it is Fairtrade?
- why you like it?

Volcanoes

What is a volcano?

1 Volcanoes look like mountains, but they are actually openings in the Earth's surface, or crust. Volcanoes can be different shapes, but inside they are all the same.

Where do you find volcanoes?

The Earth's crust is very thin and consists of large, thin
5 pieces of rock called tectonic plates. The Earth has sixteen main plates. Volcanoes are often near the places where the plates meet. The plates lie on a softer, hotter layer called the mantle and they are constantly moving. Sometimes one plate goes under another and the plate
10 melts and forms a hot liquid called magma. Because the plates are always moving, holes sometimes appear in the Earth's crust. The heat inside the Earth creates a lot of pressure and sometimes the hot magma explodes through the holes. This explosion is called a volcanic
15 eruption. The volcano is active.

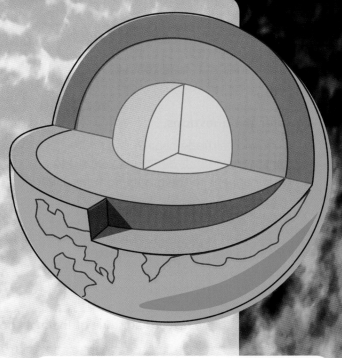

Parts of a volcano

- **Magma:** This is the hot liquid inside the volcano. It contains rock and gas.
- **Magma chamber:** This is a large underground pool. It contains the magma.
20 - **Pipe:** This is in the middle of the volcano. The magma comes out of the magma chamber and travels up the pipe, to the vent.
- **Vent:** This is the opening at the top of a volcano. The magma comes out of the vent in the form of lava.
25 - **Lava:** This is the magma in an eruption. Lava is extremely hot (700° to 1200°C).
- **Base:** This is the bottom of a volcano. Sometimes the base is on the earth's surface, sometimes it is at the bottom of the ocean.

30 There are about 1,500 active volcanoes in the world. The largest volcano is Mauna Loa in Hawaii. Its lowest part is at the bottom of the ocean. From the bottom to the top, it is about 8,700 m tall, taller than Mount Everest.

Useful language

opening (n) *line 2*
rock (n) *line 5*
layer (n) *line 8*
melt (v) *line 10*

1 How many active volcanoes are there in the world?

2 Read the text again. Label the parts of a volcano with the words in the box.

lava   magma chamber   pipe   ~~vent~~

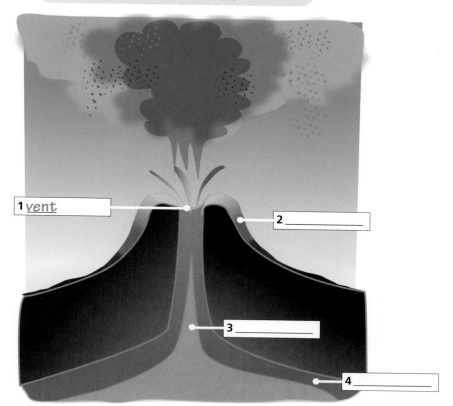

1 vent

2 _____

3 _____

4 _____

3 Answer the questions.

What are volcanoes?
Volcanoes are openings in the Earth's surface.

1 What are tectonic plates?

_____

2 Where do you find volcanoes?

_____

3 Why do holes appear in the Earth's crust?

_____

4 What happens during an eruption?

_____

5 What is the difference between magma and lava?

_____

6 What is Mauna Loa?

_____

Project

Write an article about a volcano for a geography website.
Think about the following questions:

• Where is it?
• How big is it?
• Is it active?
• When was the last eruption?
• What happened when the volcano erupted?

Word list

Unit 1

Physical descriptions

beard /bɪrd/
blond /blɑnd/
curly /'kərli/
freckle /'frɛkl/
glasses /'glæsəz/
heavy /'hɛvi/
long /lɔŋ/
mustache /'mʌstæʃ/
short /ʃɔrt/
shoulder-length /'ʃoʊldər lɛŋkθ/
slim /slɪm/
spiky /'spaɪki/
straight /streɪt/
tall /tɔl/
wavy /'weɪvi/

Nouns

article /'arʈɪkl/
championship /'tʃæmpiən,ʃɪp/
dancer /'dænsər/
dictionary /'dɪkʃə,nɛri/
driver /'draɪvər/
prize /praɪz/
radio /'reɪdioʊ/
season /'sizn/
singer /'sɪŋer/
songwriter /'sɔŋraɪʈər/
swimmer /'swɪmər/
yearbook /'yɪr ,bʊk/

Verbs

borrow /'baroʊ/
call /kɔl/
coach /koʊtʃ/
interview /'ɪntərvyu/
practice /'præktəs/
ring /rɪŋ/

Adjectives

bad /bæd/
beautiful /'byuʈəfl/
early /'ərli/
fantastic /fæn'tæstɪk/
fast /fæst/
gigantic /dʒaɪ'gæntɪk/
good /gʊd/
happy /'hæpi/
late /leɪt/
professional /prə'fɛʃənl/
quiet /'kwaɪət/
star (player) /'star (pleɪər)/

Adverbs

badly /'bædli/
beautifully /'byuʈəfli/
fantastically /fæn'tæstɪkli/
happily /'hæpəli/
quietly /'kwaɪətli/
slowly /'sloʊli/
well /wɛl/

Unit 2

Musical instruments and genres

drums /drʌms/
guitar /gɪ'tar/
harp /harp/
piano /pi'ænoʊ/
recorder /ri'kɔrdər/
saxophone /'sælksəfoʊn/
trumpet /'trʌmpət/
violin /vaɪə'lɪn/

classical /'klæsɪkl/
hip-hop /hɪp hap/
jazz /dʒæz/
pop /pap/
reggae /'rɛgeɪ/
rock /rak/

Nouns

abbreviation /ə,brivi'eɪʃn/
athlete /'æθlit/
atmosphere /'ætməsfɪr/
band /bænd/
charity /'tʃærəʈi/
concert /'kansərt/
disaster /dɪ'zæstər/
drummer /'drʌmər/
fault /fɔlt/
guitarist /gɪ'tarɪst/
human rights organization /'hyumən raɪts ,ɔrgənə'zeɪʃn/
lead singer /lid 'sɪŋer/
lyric /'lɪrɪk/
musician /myu'zɪʃn/
nickname /'nɪkneɪm/
performer /pər'fɔrmər/
project /'pradʒɛkt/
report card /rɪ'pɔrt kard/
score /skɔr/
superstar /'supərstar/
theme /θim/

Adjectives

blues /bluz/
country /'kʌntri/
electric /ɪ'lɛktrɪk/
gospel /'gaspl/
mad /mæd/
political /pə'lɪʈɪkl/
poor /pʊr/
popular /'papyələr/
rap /ræp/
rock 'n' roll /,rakn'roʊl/
social /'soʊʃl/

Review A

Adjectives

brilliant /'brɪlyənt/
talent /'tælənt/

Culture Club A

Nouns

leader /'lidər/
stadium /'steɪdiəm/

Adjectives

crazy /'kreɪzi/
enormous /ɪ'nɔrməs/
glamorous /'glæmərəs/
incredible /ɪn'krɛdəbl/
influential /,ɪnflu'ɛnʃl/
rebellious /rɪ'bɛlyəs/

Unit 3

Jobs

accountant /ə'kaʊntnt/
doctor /'daktər/
electrician /,ɪlɛk'trɪʃn/
engineer /,ɛndʒə'nɪr/
factory worker /'fæktəri 'wərkər/
hairdresser /'hɛrdrɛsər/
journalist /'dʒərnəlɪst/
lawyer /'lɔyər/
office worker /'ɔfəs wərkər/
postal worker /'poʊstl wərkər/
salesclerk /'seɪlzklɑrk/
teacher /'titʃər/

Nouns

ambition /æm'bɪʃn/
army /'armi/
bus station /'bʌs steɪʃn/
bus stop /'bʌs stap/
chance /tʃæns/
colony /'kaləni/

colonist /'kalənɪst/
commander /kə'mændər/
commerce /'kamərs/
engine /'ɛndʒən/
excuse /ɪks'kyus/
explorer /ɪk'splɔrər/
gold /goʊld/
independence /ɪndɪ'pɛndəns/
Indians /'ɪndiənz/
island /'aɪlənd/
journey /'dʒərni/
kart /kart/
letter /'lɛʈər/
machine /mə'ʃin/
office /'ɔfəs/
parcel /'parsl/
personality /,pərsə'næləʈi/
physicist /'fɪzəsɪst/
plant /plænt/
professor /prə'fɛsər/
research /'risərtʃ/
route /rut/
sailor /'seɪlər/
salon /sə'lan/
ship /ʃɪp/
writer /'raɪʈər/

Verbs

agree /ə'gri/
apologize /ə'palədʒaɪz/
arrive /ə'raɪv/
believe /bɪ'liv/
celebrate /'sɛləbreɪt/
continue /kən'tɪnyu/
cry /kraɪ/
cut /kʌt/
decide /dɪ'saɪd/
declare /dɪ'klɛr/
deliver /dɪ'lɪvər/
design /dɪ'zaɪn/
die /daɪ/
discover /dɪs'kʌvər/
end /ɛnd/
fail /feɪl/
fight /faɪt/
forget /fər'gɛt/
help /hɛlp/
join /dʒɔɪn/
make /meɪk/
marry /'mæri/
need /nid/
prefer /prɪ'fər/
race /reɪs/
return /rɪ'tərn/
sell /sɛl/
spend /spend/
style /staɪl/
use /yuz/
win /wɪn/

Adjectives

dangerous /,deɪndʒərəs/
fair /fɛr/
independent /,ɪndɪ'pɛndənt/
radioactive /,reɪdioʊ'aktɪv/
round /raʊnd/
successful /sək'sɛsfl/

Unit 4

Movies

action movie /'ækʃn muvi/
animated movie /'ænəmeɪʈəd muvi/
comedy /'kamədi/
fantasy movie /'fæntəsi muvi/
horror movie /'hɔrər muvi/
love story /'lʌv stɔri/
science fiction movie /'saɪəns fɪkʃn muvi/
thriller /'θrɪlər/

Nouns

autograph /ˈɔtəgræf/
center /ˈsɛntər/
comedian /kəˈmidiən/
credit /ˈkrɛdət/
critic /ˈkrɪtɪk/
debut /deɪˈbyu/
jeans /dʒinz/
performance /pərˈfɔrməns/
popcorn /ˈpɑpkɔrn/
premiere /priˈmɪr/
role /roʊl/
screen /skrin/
secret /ˈsikrət/
showing /ˈʃoʊɪŋ/
success /səkˈsɛs/
ticket /ˈtɪkət/
voice /vɔɪs/

Verbs

act /ækt/
appear /əˈpɪr/
bet /bɛt/
direct /dəˈrɛkt/
star /stɑr/
start /stɑrt/
surf /sərf/

Adjectives

angry /ˈæŋgri/
frightening /ˈfraɪtnɪŋ/
hot /hɑt/
natural /ˈnætʃərəl/

Review B

Nouns

blog /blɑg/
selection /səˈlɛkʃn/
souvenir /ˌsuvəˈnɪr/

Adjectives

fictional /ˈfɪkʃnl/
nervous /ˈnərvəs/
parallel /ˈpærəlɛl/
romantic /roʊˈmæntɪk/
simple /ˈsɪmpl/

Culture club B

Nouns

career /kəˈrɪr/
mouse /maʊs/
movie studio /ˈmuvi ˈstudioʊ/
show /ʃoʊ/
silent movie /ˈsaɪlənt ˈmuvi/
symbol /ˈsɪmbl/
theme park /θim pɑrk/
TV channel /ˌti vi tʃænl/

Verbs

change /tʃeɪndʒ/
create /kriˌeɪt/
suggest /səˌdʒɛst/

Unit 5

Transportation

airplane /ˈɛrpleɪn/
bike /baɪk/
boat /boʊt/
bus /bʌs/
car /kɑr/
ferry /ˈfɛri/
helicopter /ˈhɛləkɑptər/
motorcycle /ˈmoʊtərˌsaɪkl/
subway /ˈsʌbweɪ/
taxi /ˈtæksi/
train /treɪn/
truck /trʌk/

Nouns

accommodation /əˌkɑməˈdeɪʃn/
captain /ˈkæptən/
dayplanner /ˈdeɪplænər/
departure time /dɪˈpɑrtʃər taɪm/
destination /ˌdɛstəˈneɪʃn/
emu /ˈimyu/
harbor /ˈhɑrbər/
jeep /dʒip/
killer whale /ˈkɪlər weɪl/
middle /ˈmɪdl/
pain /peɪn/
pair /pɛr/
park /pɑrk/

Verbs

accept /əkˈsɛpt/
catch /kætʃ/
chase /tʃeɪs/

collect /kəˈlɛkt/
complete /kəmˈplit/
conquer /ˈkɑŋkər/
cross /krɔs/
meet /mit/
organize /ˈɔrgənaɪz/
raise /reɪz/
refuse /rɪˈfyuz/

Adjectives

constant /ˈkɑnstənt/
enormous /ɪˈnɔrməs/
free /fri/
generous /ˈdʒɛnərəs/
sharp /ʃɑrp/

Adverbs

instead /ɪnˈstɛd/
together /təˈgɛðər/

Unit 6

Food and drink

apple /ˈæpl/
beef /bif/
bread /brɛd/
carrot /ˈkærət/
cheese /tʃiz/
chicken /ˈtʃɪkən/
cookie /ˈkʊki/
egg /ɛg/
mango /ˈmæŋgoʊ/
milk /mɪlk/
orange juice /ˈɔrɪndʒ dʒus/
potato /pəˈteɪtoʊ/
rice /raɪs/
salmon /ˈsæmən/
tomato /təˈmeɪtoʊ/
tuna /ˈtunə/
water /ˈwɔtər/
yogurt /ˈyoʊgərt/

Other nouns

author /ˈɔθər/
banana /bəˈnænə/
bottle /ˈbɑtl/
carbohydrates /ˌkɑrboʊˈhaɪdreɪts/
chocolate /ˈtʃɑklət/
coffee /ˈkɔfi/
couple /ˈkʌpl/
cow /kaʊ/
cupboard /ˈkʌbərd/
dairy product /ˈdɛri ˈprɑdʌkt/
dessert /dɪˈzərt/
drink /drɪŋk/
duck /dʌk/
fast food /fæst fud/
fish /fɪʃ/
fruit /frut/
gram /græm/
habit /ˈhæbət/
ham /hæm/
hamburger /ˈhæmˈbərgər/
lamb /læm/

Nouns

lettuce /ˈlɛtəs/
meat /mit/
mousse /mus/
mutton /ˈmʌtn/
pig /pɪg/
pork /pɔrk/
portion /ˈpɔrʃn/
protein /ˈproʊtin/
recipe /ˈrɛsəpi/
refrigerator /rɪˈfrɪdʒəreɪtər/
sandwich /ˈsænwɪtʃ/
sheep /ʃip/
soda /ˈsoʊdə/
snack /snæk/
tea /ti/
teenager /ˈtineɪdʒər/
vegetable /ˈvɛdʒtəbl/

Verbs

buy /baɪ/
cook /kʊk/
hate /heɪt/
know /noʊ/
moan /moʊn/
order /ˈɔrdər/
offer /ˈɔfər/

Adjectives

baked /beɪkt/
funny /ˈfʌni/
healthy /ˈhɛlθi/
hungry /ˈhʌngri/
normal /ˈnɔrml/
roast /roʊst/
simple /ˈsɪmpl/
unhealthy /ʌnˈhɛlθi/

Adverbs

already /ɔˈrɛdi/

Review C

Nouns

sugar /ˈʃʊgər/
tour /tʊr/

Adjectives

surprise /sərˈpraɪz/

Culture club C

Nouns

burger /ˈbərgər/
chain /tʃeɪn/
fries /fraɪz/
memorabilia /ˌmɛmərəˈbiliə/
museum /myuˈziəm/
personal possession /ˈpərsənl pəˈzɛʃn/

Unit 7

Geography

continent /ˈkɑntənənt/
country /ˈkʌntri/
desert /ˈdɛzərt/
island /ˈaɪlənd/
lake /leɪk/
mountain /ˈmaʊntn/
ocean /ˈoʊʃn/
river /ˈrɪvər/
sea /si/
volcano /vɑlˈkeɪnoʊ/

Nouns

assistant /əˈsɪstənt/
average /ˈævrɪdʒ/
bite /baɪt/
chimpanzee /ˈtʃɪmpænˈzi/
climate /ˈklaɪmət/
diet /ˈdaɪət/
disease /dɪˈziz/
dolphin /ˈdɑlfən/
inhabitant /ɪnˈhæbətənt/
kangaroo /ˌkæŋgəˈru/

Word list

pattern /ˈpæʧərn/
pet /pɛt/
rodent /ˈroʊdnt/
tarantula /təˈrænʧələ/
temperature /ˈtɛmprəʧər/
tiger /ˈtaɪgər/

Verbs

advise /ədˈvaɪz/
belong /bɪˈlɔŋ/
weigh /weɪ/

Adjectives

active /ˈæktɪv/
aggressive /əˈgrɛsɪv/
big /bɪg/
bizarre /bɪˈzar/
cheap /ʧip/
exotic /ɪgˈzɑʈɪk/
expensive /ɪkˈspɛnsɪv/
friendly /ˈfrɛndli/
hard /hard/
high /haɪ/
hopeless /ˈhoʊpləs/
impressed /ɪmˈprɛst/
intelligent /ɪnˈtɛlədʒənt/
long /lɔŋ/
nocturnal /nɑkˈtərnl/
poisonous /ˈpɔɪznəs/
safe /seɪf/
smart /smɑrt/
strange /streɪndʒ/
talented /ˈtæləntəd/
volcanic /vɑlˈkænɪk/

Unit 8

Feelings and emotions

angry /ˈæŋgri/
annoyed /əˈnɔɪd/
bored /bɔrd/
confident /ˈkɑnfədənt/
embarrassed /ɪmˈbærəst/
excited /ɪkˈsaɪʈəd/
fed up /ˌfɛdˈʌp/
frightened /ˈfraɪtnd/
happy /ˈhæpi/
nervous /ˈnərvəs/
proud /praʊd/
sad /sæd/

Nouns

bride /braɪd/
chemical /ˈkɛmɪkl/
crocodile /ˈkrɑkədaɪl/
culture /ˈkʌlʧər/
elephant /ˈɛləfənt/
emotion /ɪˈmoʊʃn/
fortune /ˈfɔrʧən/
funeral /ˈfyunərəl/
giraffe /dʒəˈræf/
happiness /ˈhæpinəs/
hormone /ˈhɔrmoʊn/
host /hoʊst/
kilometer /kɪˈlɑmɪəʈər/
memory /ˈmɛməri/
message /ˈmɛsɪdʒ/
mile /maɪl/
peace /pis/
peregrine falcon /pɛrəgrɪn ˈfælkən/
purity /ˈpyʊrəʈi/

Verbs

affect /əˈfɛkt/
control /kənˈtroʊl/
feel /fil/
improve /ɪmˈpruv/
influence /ˈɪnfluəns/
receive /rɪˈsiv/
relax /rɪˈlæks/
return /rɪˈtərn/
symbolize /ˈsɪmbəlaɪz/

Adjectives

busy /ˈbɪzi/
calm /kɑm/
close /kloʊs/
impatient /ɪmˈpeɪʃnt/
irritable /ˈɪrəʈəbl/
negative /ˈnɛgəʈɪv/
noisy /ˈnɔɪzi/
positive /ˈpɑzəʈɪv/
ready /ˈrɛdi/
relaxing /rɪˈlæksɪŋ/
rich /rɪʧ/
worried /ˈwərid/

Adverbs

definitely /ˈdɛfənətli/

Review D

Nouns

alligator /ˈæləgeɪʈər/
flower /ˈflaʊər/
goldfish /ˈgoʊldfɪʃ/
result /rɪˈzʌlt/

Adjectives

populated /ˈpɑpyəˌleɪʈɪd/
related /rɪˌleɪˈʈəd/

Culture club D

Nouns

barbecue /ˈbɑrbɪkyu/
fanatic /fəˈnæʈɪk/
karaoke /ˌkæriˈoʊki/
natural world /ˈnæʧərəl wərld/
world record /wərld ˈrɛkərd/

Curriculum extra A

Nouns

baton /bəˈtɑn/
conductor /kənˈdʌktər/
orchestra /ˈɔrkəstrə/
percussionist /pərˈkʌʃnɪst/
stage /steɪdʒ/
strings /strɪŋ/

Adjectives

brass /bræs/
chamber /ˈʧeɪmbər/
percussion /pərˈkʌʃn/
symphony /ˈsɪmfəni/
woodwind /ˈwʊdwɪnd/

Curriculum extra B

Nouns

animation /ˈænəˈmeɪʃn/
animator /ˈænəˌmeɪʈər/
cel /sɛl/
frame /freɪm/
glass disk /glæs dɪsk/
model /ˈmɑdl/
object /ˈɑbdʒɛkt/
project /prəˈdʒɛkt/
projector /prəˈdʒɛktər/
stop-frame animation /ˈstɑp freɪm ˌænəˈmeɪʃn/
technique /tɛkˈnik/
version /ˈvərʃn/
zoopraxiscope /zuˈprækskoʊp/

Adjectives

complicated /ˈkɑmpləkeɪʈəd/
computer-generated /kəmˈpyuʈər ˈdʒɛnə reɪʈəd/
plastic /ˈplæstɪk/
three-dimensional /θri dəˈmɛnʃnl/

Curriculum extra C

Nouns

business organization /ˈbɪznəs ˌɔrgənəˈzeɪʃn/
company /ˈkʌmpəni/
co-operative /koʊˈɑprəʈɪv/
crop /krɑp/
farm /fɑrm/
market /ˈmɑrkət/
poverty /ˈpɑvərʈi/
profit /ˈprɑfət/
supermarket /ˈsupərmɑrkət/

Verbs

produce /prəˈdus/

Adjectives

Fairtrade /ˈfɛr treɪd/
fixed price /fɪkst praɪs/
international /ˌɪntərˈnæʃənl/
local /ˌloʊkl/

Curriculum extra D

Nouns

chamber /ˈʧeɪmbər/
crust /krʌst/
hole /hoʊl/
lava /ˈlɑvə/
layer /ˈleɪər/
magma /ˈmɑgmə/
opening /ˈoʊpənɪŋ/
pipe /paɪp/
rock /rɑk/
shape /ʃeɪp/
tectonic plate /tɛkˈtɑnɪk pleɪt/
vent /vɛnt/

Got it!

Level 1
Workbook

Philippa Bowen & Denis Delaney

1 Grammar rules

Simple present / Present progressive
Simple present

	Affirmative	Negative
I	play	don't play
you	play	don't play
he / she / it	plays	doesn't play
we / you / they	play	don't play

Affirmative

Subject +	base form of the verb	(+ -s with the third person singular)

Negative

Subject +	do not / does not don't / doesn't	+ base form of the verb

Interrogative	Short answers	
	Affirmative	Negative
Do I **play**?	Yes, you **do**.	No, you **don't**.
Do you **play**?	Yes, I **do**.	No, I **don't**.
Does he / she / it **play**?	Yes, he / she / it **does**.	No, he / she / it **doesn't**.
Do we / you / they **play**?	Yes, we / you / they **do**.	No, we / you / they **don't**.

Do / Does + subject + base form of the verb?
Yes, + subject pronoun + *do / does*.
No, + subject pronoun + *don't / doesn't*.

1 **We use the simple present to talk about habits**
   I **get up** at half past seven.

2 **We use adverbs of frequency to say how often something happens.**
   100% ——————————————— 0%
   always usually often sometimes rarely never
   I **usually** do my homework in the afternoon.
   Other expressions of frequency
   every day / month   twice a day / month
   once a day / month   three times a day / month

Spelling variations

1 **We make the third person singular with the base form of the verb + -s.**
   like + **-s**   like**s**

2 **We use the base form of the verb + -es when the verb ends in -ch, -s, -sh, -x, -z, or -o.**
   he teach**es**   she go**es**   it wash**es**

3 **When the verb ends in a consonant + -y, we change the -y to -i and add -es.**
   she stud**ies**   it fl**ies**

4 **When the verb ends in a vowel + -y we add -s.**
   he play**s**

Present progressive

	Affirmative	Negative
I	'm playing	'm not playing
you	're playing	aren't playing
he / she / it	's playing	isn't playing
we / you / they	're playing	aren't playing

Subject +	am ('m) is ('s) + not are ('re)	+ base form of the verb + -ing

Questions	Short answers	
	Affirmative	Negative
Am I **playing**?	Yes, you **are**.	No, you **aren't**.
Are you **playing**?	Yes, I **am**.	No, I**'m not**.
Is he / she / it **playing**?	Yes, he / she / it **is**.	No, he / she / it **isn't**.
Are we / you / they **playing**?	Yes, we / you / they **are**.	No, we / you / they **aren't**.

Am + *Is* + *Are* +	subject	+ base form of the verb + -ing

Yes, + *No,* +	subject pronoun + subject pronoun +	am / is / are. 'm not / isn't / aren't.

1 **We use the present progressive to talk about something that is happening now.**
   He**'s playing** basketball at the moment.

2 **We often use these expressions with the present progressive:**
   now   at the moment   today   this week

Spelling variations

1 **For most verbs we add -ing to the base form.**
   play + **-ing** = **playing**   walk + **-ing** = **walking**

2 When the verb ends in -*e*, we drop the -*e* and add -*ing*.

have ⟶ **having**

3 For short verbs ending in a vowel plus a consonant, we double the final consonant and add -*ing*.

sit ⟶ **sitting**

4 *Travel* is irregular.

travel ⟶ **traveling**

Possessive pronouns

Possessive adjectives	Possessive pronouns
my	mine
your	yours
his	his
her	hers
its	–
our	ours
your	yours
their	theirs

1 Possessive adjectives come before a noun.

my DVD player   **your** pencil

2 Possessive pronouns substitute a possessive adjective and a noun.

It's **my** DVD player. = It's **mine**.

3 We often use possessive pronouns to avoid repeating.

This is **my pen**. That's **your pen**. That's **yours**.

4 We usually make possessive pronouns by adding -*s* to the possessive adjective.

They're **her** CDs. They're **hers**.
mine and *his* are irregular.
It's **my** bag. It's **mine**.
It's **his** MP3 player. It's **his**.

Adverbs of manner
Regular adverbs

Adjective		Adverb
quick		quick**ly**
slow		slow**ly**
quiet	+ -**ly**	quiet**ly**
beautiful		beautiful**ly**
easy		eas**ily**
fantastic		fantastic**ally**

1 We use adverbs of manner to talk about how we do something. They change what the verb means.

John works **quickly**.

2 Adverbs of manner always come after a verb or after an object.

subject + verb + (object) + adverb of manner
Kate speaks **quietly**.

3 We make adverbs of manner by adding -*ly* to the adjective.

bad ⟶ bad**ly**   slow ⟶ slow**ly**

Spelling variations

1 When the adjective ends in a -*y*, we change the -*y* to -*i* and add -*ly*.

easy ⟶ eas**ily**   noisy ⟶ nois**ily**

2 When the adjective ends in -*ic*, we add –*ally*.

fantastic ⟶ fantastic**ally**

Irregular adverbs

Adjective	Adverb
good	well
early	early
late	late
fast	fast

• Irregular adjectives do not follow any rules.

Word list

Physical descriptions

beard _____   long _____
eyes _____   mustache _____
freckles _____   short _____
glasses _____   slim _____
heavy _____   tall _____

Hair

black _____   short _____
blond _____   shoulder-length _____
brown _____   spiky _____
curly _____   straight _____
long _____   wavy _____
red _____

Student Book pp. 12–13, p.15

Exercises

Physical descriptions

1 Circle the odd word out.

tall   short   (wavy)

1 curly   spiky   brown
2 mustache   heavy   beard
3 tall   shoulder-length   long
4 blond   blue   green
5 short   slim   freckles

2 Choose the correct answers.

Mr. Jones is a **long** / (**tall**) man.

1 Jayne wears **freckles** / **glasses**.
2 John has a mustache and a short **beard** / **hair**.
3 My mom has blond **eyes** / **hair**.
4 Tina's very **slim** / **spiky**.
5 I have short, **shoulder-length** / **curly** hair.
6 Martin has a **long** / **tall** face.

3 Copy and complete the factfile for three members of your family and your best friend. Then write sentences.

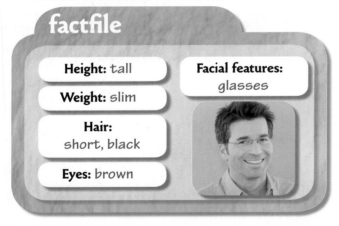

factfile

Height: tall

Weight: slim

Hair: short, black

Eyes: brown

Facial features: glasses

My dad is tall and slim. He has short black hair and brown eyes. He wears glasses.

Simple present / Present progressive

4 Choose the correct answers.

I often (**go**) / **am going** swimming.
Tom is reading a book **every evening** / (**at the moment**).

1 Dad usually **cooks** / **is cooking** dinner on Sunday.

2 Rob and Daniel are playing chess **now** / **once a month**.
3 We **are going** / **go** bowling every Friday evening.
4 **Do you always play** / **Are you always playing** volleyball on the weekend?
5 I don't watch TV **today** / **every day**.
6 Mom **doesn't work** / **isn't working** today. She's on vacation.

5 Write sentences. Use the correct form of the simple present or present progressive.

Ellie / go to school on Saturdays (✗)
Ellie doesn't go to school on Saturdays.
John / take a shower / at the moment (?)
Is John taking a shower at the moment?

1 Sue / go shopping / three times a week (✓)
2 Jack / watch the movie / at the moment (?)
3 Julie / speak German (?)
4 they / study / at the moment (✗)
5 the phone / ring / now (✓)
6 you / usually / come to school by bus (?)
7 I / use / the computer / at the moment (✗)
8 Tom / play tennis / on Mondays (?)

6 Complete the dialogues with the correct form of the words in parentheses.

A Where's Tom? <u>What's he doing</u>? (he / do)
B He's in his bedroom. He<u>'s listening</u> (listen) to music.

1 A How often _____ (Karen / go) swimming?
  B Four times a week! She _____ (like) swimming a lot!

2 A _____ (the boys / use) the Internet at the moment?
  B Yes, they are. They _____ (write) an e-mail to Grandma.

3 A What _____ (you / do) in the evenings?
  B I usually _____ (play) computer games or I _____ (watch) TV.

4 A What _____ (Mom / do)?
  B She _____ (cook) dinner.

Possessive pronouns

7 Complete the chart.

Possessive adjectives	Possessive pronouns
my	mine
your	3 _____
1 _____	his
her	4 _____
its	–
our	5 _____
your	6 _____
2 _____	theirs

8 Complete the sentences with the possessive adjective or possessive pronoun.

"Is this your cell phone?" "No, it isn't **mine**."
This is my sister. **Her** name's Michelle.

1 "Are these your keys, Kevin?"
"Yes, they're _____. Thanks."
2 Megan and Paul are Canadian. _____ dad's from Toronto.
3 This isn't Ellen's rucksack! _____ is pink.
4 Here's your DVD. And are these _____, too?
5 Oxford is famous for _____ university.
6 These aren't our skis! _____ are new!

Adverbs of manner

9 Complete the chart.

Adjectives	Adverb
quiet	_quietly_
slow	1 _____
quick	2 _____
bad	3 _____
early	4 _____
happy	5 _____
good	6 _____

10 Complete the sentences. Use words from exercise 9.

The baby's sleeping. Please talk **quietly**.

1 Peter's very intelligent. He usually finishes his homework _____.
2 Tortoises walk very _____.
3 Dad starts work at 7 a.m., so he always gets up _____.
4 Your handwriting's terrible! You write really _____.

5 Philip loves piano lessons. He always plays really _____.
6 My baby sister's great. She always smiles _____.

Round-up

11 Choose the correct answers.

Jayne is a (beautiful)/ beautifully singer.

1 I'm eating a pizza **every Friday / at the moment.**
2 How often **are you going / do you go** to the movies?
3 "Is that your book, Anna?" "Yes, it's **my / mine.**"
4 The school basketball team usually plays **good / well.**
5 Are these **your / yours** books?
6 We visit our grandparents **now / once a week.**

12 Choose the correct answers.

Hi, Emma!
I ¹ **write / 'm writing** to you from Dallas! I'm on vacation here with my family. Dallas, Texas, is in the U.S. and it has a very multicultural population. About 35% ² **speak / are speaking** Spanish. I can't speak Spanish very ³ **good / well**, but the receptionist in our hotel is teaching me some expressions. It's fun! I'm also learning some new American words. In Texas, for example, they ⁴ **don't say / aren't saying** "hello" or "hi", they say "howdy". It's really cool!
There are a lot of museums here – ⁵ **our / ours** favorite is The Firefighters Museum.
We always get up early, have breakfast ⁶ **quick / quickly** and then take a bus to a new location. In the evenings, we usually ⁷ **go / are going** to a different restaurant. My dad's favorite restaurant here is Spanish, but ⁸ **my / mine** is the American restaurant TGIF.
At the moment we ⁹ **relax / are relaxing** in the hotel. Dad ¹⁰ **reads / is reading** the newspaper and Mom is sleeping!
I really love Dallas and I don't want to come home! What ¹¹ **do you do / are you doing** at the moment?
Bye!
Andy

Communication

Making requests

1 Complete the dialogues with the phrases below.

> Can I borrow   Can I have   ~~Can I open~~
> I'm doing   Not now   you can   you can't

1
A <u>Can I open</u> the window, please?
B Yes, [1]_____. It's hot in here.
A Thank you.

2
A [2]_____ your English dictionary, Susana?
B [3]_____. [4]_____ my homework. You can borrow it later.

3
A [5]_____ an ice cream, Mom?
B No, [6]_____! It's nearly dinner time.

2 Match the questions with the answers.

1 Can I have a sandwich, Mom? I'm hungry.   [b]
2 Can I use your pen, please?   ☐
3 Can I borrow your Exodus CD?   ☐
4 Can I watch this movie, Dad?   ☐
5 Can I have that computer, Mom?   ☐
6 Can I go out on my bike?   ☐

a No, you can't. It's time for bed.
b ~~Yes, you can. There's some ham in the fridge.~~
c Not now. Grandma's here. You can go out later.
d Yes, you can. Here you are.
e Not now. I'm listening to it.
f No, you can't! You have a computer.

3 Complete the dialogue with the words below.

> Can I close   ~~Can I have~~   Can I use
> Can I wear   No, you can't   Not now
> Yes, you can   You can use it later

<u>Can I have</u> an apple, please?
Yes, you can. The fruit is in the bowl.

1 A [1]_____ your jacket to the party, Sophie?
  B [2]_____! I want to wear it.
2 A [3]_____ your CD player, Tim?
  B [4]_____. I'm using it for my homework. [5]_____.

3 A [6]_____ the window, please?
  B [7]_____. It's cold in here.
  A Thank you.

4 Use the instructions to write requests and answers.

Ask your teacher if you can borrow her dictionary.
Can I borrow your dictionary?
She replies positively.
Yes, you can.

1 Ask your friend if you can read her journal.
_____

She replies negatively.
_____

2 Ask your dad if you can use his cell phone.
_____

He says no because he's waiting for an important phone call.
_____

3 Ask your mom if you can have a snack.
_____

She replies positively.
_____

4 Ask your brother if you can borrow his MP3 player.
_____

He says no, but that you can borrow it later.
_____

5 Use the instructions to write dialogues.

1 You go into a busy fast food restaurant. A woman is sitting at a small table but there's an empty seat next to her. You ask her if you can sit down. She agrees.
You   _____
Woman _____

2 You are staying with a family in England and you want to watch a DVD. You ask your host if you can use the DVD player. Your host says that you can't because dinner is ready, but that you can use it later.
You   _____
Your host _____

3 You need a calculator in class but yours is at home. You ask your friend if you can borrow his. He agrees and gives it to you.
You   _____
Your friend _____

Reading

Learn English in the U.S.

Every year students from all over the world come to the U.S. to learn English. They have English lessons at a language school but they often live with a host family. Seong is sixteen and she's on a study vacation in Boston. Here she talks about her experience.

"Hi! My name's Seong Hye Park and I come from Seoul in South Korea. At the moment, I'm visiting the U.S. I'm here on a study vacation and I'm staying in Boston, Massachusetts. It's on the east coast.

Boston is a pretty and historic city. It has a lot of green parks and beautiful architecture. It's also the home of Harvard University. That's a really old and important university in the States.

I'm staying with a host family. There are four people in the family – Mr. and Mrs. Taylor and their children Sophie and Jack. Sophie's fifteen and she's cool. Jack is only four years old. He has blue eyes and blond, curly hair. He's cute!

I go to my language school five days a week and I have lessons from 9 a.m. to 1 p.m. The other students in my class are from South America, China, and Europe. We always talk in English! It's great fun and I'm learning a lot!"

1 **Read the text. Then answer the questions.**

1 What nationality is Seong Hye?

_____

2 What is she doing in Boston?

_____

3 What is Boston like?

_____

4 Who is she staying with?

_____

5 What does Jack look like?

_____

6 How often does she go to her language school?

_____

7 Where do the other students come from?

_____

8 What language do they use to communicate?

_____

Writing

2 **Imagine that you are on a study vacation to learn English in the U.S. Write an e-mail about it to a friend. Use these questions to help you.**

- Where is the language school?
- What is the city like?
- What's the name of your host family?
- How many people are there in the family?
- What are their names?
- What do the children look like?
- When do you have lessons?
- What do you do in the evenings?
- Are you enjoying your stay? Why?

> Hi, Felipe
> Hello from _____! I'm staying here to learn English. The city …

be: Simple past
Affirmative

Affirmative
I **was**
you **were**
he **was**
she **was**
it **was**
we **were**
you **were**
they **were**

Subject + *was* / *were*

1. We use *was* with singular pronouns and singular nouns. We use *were* with plural pronouns and plural nouns.

2. We do not contract *was* and *were*.

3. We use the simple past to talk about situations in the past.

be: Simple past
Negative

Negative	
Full forms	**Short forms**
I **was not**	I **wasn't**
you **were not**	you **weren't**
he **was not**	he **wasn't**
she **was not**	she **wasn't**
it **was not**	it **wasn't**
we **were not**	we **weren't**
you **were not**	you **weren't**
they **were not**	they **weren't**

Subject + | was not / were not / | wasn't / weren't |

1. **We make the negative with *was* / *were* + *not*.**
   He **was not** at school.
   The books **were not** on the desk.

2. We can use the short forms *wasn't* and *weren't*.
   I **wasn't** at home.
   You **weren't** at the concert.

3. We usually use the short forms *wasn't* and *weren't* in spoken English and when we write e-mails or letters to friends.

Past time expressions

Past time expressions
yesterday morning / afternoon / evening
last night / Monday / week / month / year
a year / a month / a week / 2 days / 20 minutes **ago**

1. We use these time expressions to say when something happened in the past.
   Yesterday morning, I was late for school.
   Last month, we were in Spain.
   We were in Rome **two weeks ago.**

2. We can put the time expressions at the start or end of the sentence. The meaning does not change.
   Yesterday morning, / Last month, / Two weeks ago, the students were on a school trip.
   The students were on a school trip **yesterday morning / last month / two weeks ago.**

be: Simple past
Interrogative and short answers

Interrogative	Short answers	
	Affirmative	**Negative**
Was I?	Yes, you **were**.	No, you **weren't**.
Were you?	Yes, I **was**.	No, I **wasn't**.
Was he?	Yes, he **was**.	No, he **wasn't**.
Was she?	Yes, she **was**.	No, she **wasn't**.
Was it?	Yes, it **was**.	No, it **wasn't**.
Were we?	Yes, you **were**.	No, you **weren't**.
Were you?	Yes, we **were**.	No, we **weren't**.
Were they?	Yes, they **were**.	No, they **weren't**.

Was / Were + subject + ... ?
Yes, + subject pronoun + *was / were*.
No, + subject pronoun + *wasn't / weren't*.

1 **We put *was* or *were* before the subject to make a question.**
Were you at the basketball game?
Was he at home yesterday?

2 **We answer questions with *Yes* + subject pronoun + *was* or *were*. The affirmative short answer has no short form.**
Were you at the concert? **Yes, I was.**
Was he in the classroom? **Yes, he was.**

3 **We answer questions with *No*, + subject pronoun + *wasn't* or *weren't*. The negative short answer has a short form.**
Was she American? **No, she wasn't.**
Were they expensive? **No, they weren't.**

Question words + *was / were*

Question word	*was / were ...*
When	were you in hospital?
Why	was he late?
Where	was she last night?
How	was the party?
How old	was she in 2004?

- **We make questions with question word + simple past of *be*.**
When was the party?
Where were you yesterday?

Watch out!

was / were born
- **We use *was / were* + *born* to talk about birth.**
When were you born?
Not ~~When are you born?~~

Word list

Musical genres and instruments
drums _____
guitar _____
harp _____
piano _____
recorder _____
saxophone _____
trumpet _____
violin _____

classical _____
hip-hop _____
jazz _____
pop _____
reggae _____
rock _____

Musicians
guitarist _____
harpist _____
trumpeter _____
violinist _____

Vocabulary

Musical genres and instruments

1 Look at the pictures and complete the puzzle. What is the secret word?

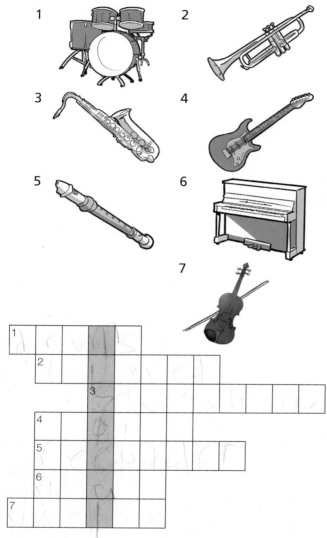

1
2
3
4
5
6
7

2 Write the name of the person who plays the musical instrument.

guitar _guitarist_   2 harp _____
1 violin _____   3 trumpet _____

Grammar

be: Simple past
Affirmative

3 Choose the correct answers.

The jazz concert (was)/ were excellent.

1 I **was / were** in Japan in 2009.
2 We **was / were** at the movies last night.

3 My parents **was / were** in New York last year.
4 John **was / were** late for school yesterday.
5 You **was / were** very happy last week.
6 My grandma **was / were** a good singer.

4 Rewrite the sentences with the simple past.

The English test is difficult.
The English test was difficult.
1 Paul and Amy are at the movies.
2 The dog's in the garden.
3 The tickets are very expensive.
4 I'm a student at Northwood School.
5 We're very tired.
6 You're late for your music lesson.

be: Simple past
Negative

5 Complete the sentences with *wasn't* or *weren't*.

Jimi Hendrix **wasn't** a jazz guitarist.

1 I _____ at soccer training last week.
2 You _____ late yesterday.
3 Pete and Andy _____ at home last night.
4 The Beach Boys _____ from Canada.
5 Daniel Craig _____ in *Die Another Day*.
6 Pelé _____ a basketball player.
7 We _____ at Sam's party.
8 The lesson _____ very interesting.

Past time expressions

6 Complete the chart with words below.

a̶ ̶y̶e̶a̶r̶   afternoon   evening
Saturday   ten minutes   three days   week

yesterday morning, yesterday [1]_____, yesterday [2]_____
last night, last [3]_____, last [4]_____
a year ago, a week ago, [5]_____ ago, [6]_____ ago

7 Write sentences. Use the affirmative or negative form of *be*.

Jack / at basketball training / last night (✓)
Jack was at basketball training last night.

1 Jack and I / at Ian's party / last Friday (✗)

_____

2 Jack and I / at school / yesterday morning (✓)

_____

3 Jack / on vacation in Mexico / last summer (✓)

_____

4 Jack / in the library / ten minutes ago (✗)

_____

5 Jack / in his bedroom / an hour ago (✗)

_____

6 Jack and Emma / at the gym / yesterday afternoon (✓)

_____

8 Rewrite the sentences from exercise 7 in chronological order.

1 Jack was in the library ten minutes ago.

be: Simple past
Interrogative and short answers

9 Write questions and answers.

The concert / good? (✓)
Was the concert good?
Yes, it was.
David / in your class last year?
(✗ / in a different school)
Was David in your class last year?
No, he wasn't. He was in a different school.

1 Ben / at the pizzeria on Friday night? (✓)
2 Luciano Pavarotti / a famous blues singer?
(✗ / opera singer)
3 English test / easy? (✗ / difficult)
4 documentary / on the radio? (✗ / the TV)
5 Saturday / December 1st? (✗ / December 2nd)
6 Peter and Jim / at school today? (✓)

Question words + *was / were*

10 Look at Oliver's journal for last week. Complete the questions and answers.

Sunday:	swimming pool with Jeff and Tim
Monday:	movies with Rachel and Patrick
Tuesday:	grandparents' house with Mom and Dad
Wednesday:	soccer practice
Thursday:	chess club with Patrick
Friday:	Lakeside shopping mall with Rachel
Saturday:	Tim's house for his birthday party

<u>Where were Oliver and his friends on Sunday?</u>
They were at the swimming pool.

1 _____?
They were at the movies.
2 _____?
On Tuesday.
3 Where was Oliver on Wednesday?
_____
4 _____
on Thursday?
They _____.
5 _____?
He was with Rachel.
6 _____?
He was at Tim's house on Saturday because it was Tim's birthday.

Round-up

11 Choose the correct answers.

Laura   Hi! Where was / (were) you last week?
You ¹ were / weren't at home.
Maria   No, I ² was / were outside the MTV awards in Bogotá.
Laura   Wow! ³ Was / Were it exciting?
Maria   Yes, it ⁴ was / were. There ⁵ was / were lots of stars and musicians.
Laura   Who ⁶ was / were there? ⁷ Was / Were your favorite ⁸ guitar / guitarist Pete Wentz there?
Maria   No, he ⁹ was / wasn't. He ¹⁰ was / wasn't in California. But Shakira and Nelly Furtado ¹¹ was / were there. It ¹² was / were cool.

Agreeing and disagreeing

1 Put the dialogue in the correct order.

Emi	And I like Tokio Hotel, too.	☐
Luke	So do I. I think they're fantastic.	☐
Emi	I like 30 Seconds to Mars.	1
Luke	Really? I do. She's great.	☐
Emi	Look, it's Katy Perry. I don't like her.	☐
Emi	And I don't like Daniela Mercury.	☐
Luke	Neither do I.	☐
Luke	Really? I don't.	☐

2 Use the prompts to complete the dialogue (✓ = agree, ✗ = disagree).

A I like Ibrahim Ferrer.
B (✓) _Me too_. I think he is fantastic.

1 I like jazz.
   (✗) _____. I think it's boring.
2 A I love opera.
   B (✗) _____. I hate opera and classical music.
3 A I don't like reggae.
   B (✓) _____. I think it's great.
4 A I like Tiziano Ferro.
   B (✗) _____. His new song's horrible!
   A I think it's fantastic!

3 Use the information to complete the dialogue.

	Louise	Peter
listening to music	☺	☺
classical music	☺	☹
rock	☹	☺
blues and jazz	☹	☺
pop	☺	☺
Akon	☹	☺

Peter   What do you like doing in your free time, Louise?
Louise I like listening to music.
Peter   So do I. What type of music do you like?
Louise I ¹_____ classical music.
Peter   ²_____. It's boring.
Louise It isn't boring. It's beautiful. What type of music do you like?
Peter   I ³_____ rock music.
Louise Really? I don't. Do you like other types of music?
Peter   Well, I ⁴_____ blues and jazz.
Louise ⁵_____. Do you like pop music?
Peter   It's OK.
Louise Who's your favorite pop singer?
Peter   ⁶_____ Akon.
Louise ⁷_____! His new song is horrible.

4 Complete the dialogue with information for you. Agree or disagree with Joe and express opinions.

Joe I really like jazz. I think it's cool!
You ¹_____
Joe I don't like folk music. It's boring.
You ²_____
Joe I love pop music. It's fantastic!
You ³_____
Joe My favorite singer's Paulina Rubio. I love her.
You ⁴_____
Joe I don't like rock music. It's horrible.
You ⁵_____
Joe I quite like classical music and opera. They're relaxing.
You ⁶_____

Reading

Music makes a difference

July 13th, 1985 was an important day in the history of pop music. It was the date of Live Aid – the first global music event for charity. There were four big concerts in different cities around the world – London, Philadelphia, Moscow and Sydney. The concerts were on television in 160 countries and there were millions of television viewers. The Live Aid concerts were to help people in Africa. In 1985 there was a famine in Ethiopia and thousands of people were hungry. The organizers, two British singers, were friends with a lot of famous pop stars. U2, Queen, Elton John, Madonna, and Bob Dylan were all at the concerts.

Live Aid was a big success and there were millions of donations for Africa – with a total of about $63 million!

Big charity music events are now common all over the world. On May 17th, 2008, Latin American singers, including Shakira, Ricky Martin and Alejandro Sanz were at two simultaneous concerts in Buenos Aires and Mexico City. The concerts were to help poor children in Latin America and were part of a project called ALAS (Latin America in Solidarity Action). The reaction to the concerts was incredible and there were donations of more than $200 million!

1 Complete the chart.

Event	When	Where	Donations
1 _____	3 _____	5 _____	7 _____
2 _____	4 _____	6 _____	8 _____

2 Answer the questions.

1 What was the aim of the Live Aid concerts?
2 What nationality were the organizers?
3 What famous pop stars were at the concerts?
4 What was the aim of the ALAS concerts in Latin America?
5 What famous Latin American stars were at the concerts?

Writing

3 Use the information in the factfile to write a paragraph about Ricky Martin.

Ricky Martin is a famous Latin American singer, songwriter, and actor. His full name is …

☆ **star factfile** ☆

Ricky Martin
Job:
singer / songwriter / actor

Full name:
Enrique Martin Morales

Date of birth:
December 24th, 1971

Place of birth:
San Juan, Pueto Rico

First international hit:
Livin' La Vida Loca

Famous songs:
She's All I Ever Had, Maria, La Copa De La Vida

Grammar rules

Simple past: Regular verbs
Affirmative

Affirmative
I walk**ed**
you walk**ed**
he walk**ed**
she walk**ed**
it walk**ed**
we walk**ed**
you walk**ed**
they walk**ed**

Base form + -ed
walk ⟶ walk**ed**

1 We make the simple past with the base form of the verb + **-ed**.
2 The simple past regular verbs have the same ending for all people.
3 We use the simple past to describe an action that started and finished in the past.
  I watch**ed** the new James Bond movie last night.

Simple past: Regular verbs
Spelling variations

1 We usually form the simple past by adding **-ed** to the base verb.

2 However, there are some spelling variations:
  – **verbs ending in -e. Add -d**
  phone ⟶ phone**d**
  arrive ⟶ arrive**d**
  – **verbs ending in -y. Change -y to -i and add -ed**
  tidy ⟶ tid**ied**
  hurry ⟶ hurr**ied**
  study ⟶ stud**ied**
  try ⟶ tr**ied**
  cry ⟶ cr**ied**
  – **short verbs ending in a vowel plus a consonant. Double the final consonant and add -ed**
  stop ⟶ stop**ped**
  rob ⟶ rob**bed**
  plan ⟶ plan**ned**
  prefer ⟶ prefer**red**
  – **_travel_ is irregular**
  travel ⟶ **traveled**

Pronunciation

1 **When the base form of the verb ends with a voiced (hard) sound, -ed is pronounced /d/.**
  rai**n**ed /reɪnd/
  lo**v**ed /lʌvd/
  pla**y**ed /pleɪd/

2 **When the base form of the verb ends with an unvoiced (soft) sound, -ed is pronounced /t/.**
  wa**tch**ed /wɑtʃt/
  li**k**ed /laɪkt/
  sto**pp**ed /stɑpt/

3 **When the base form of the verb ends with sound /d/ or /t/, -ed is pronounced /ɪd/.**
  star**t**ed /stɑrtɪd/
  ha**t**ed /heɪtɪd/
  deci**d**ed /dɪsaɪdɪd/

Simple past: Irregular verbs

1 Irregular verbs don't follow a pattern. You need to learn them.

I **go** to the movie theater every night.
→ I **went** to the movie theater last night.

2 We can put irregular verbs into groups with the same sound or spelling. This can help us to remember them.

Base form	Simple past
run	ran
drink	drank
sing	sang
sit	sat
begin	began

Base form	Simple past
buy	bo**ught**
catch	ca**ught**
teach	ta**ught**

Base form	Simple past
break	br**oke**
choose	ch**ose**
speak	sp**oke**

Base form	Simple past
cut	cut
hit	hit
put	put

Base form	Simple past
tell	t**old**
sell	s**old**

Base form	Simple past
come	came
become	became

Base form	Simple past
give	gave
forgive	forgave

Base form	Simple past
blow	blew
know	knew
grow	grew

3 The simple past irregular verbs have the same ending for all people.

I **ate** a sandwich for lunch.
He **ate** a sandwich for lunch.
They **ate** a sandwich for lunch.

4 There is a list of irregular verbs on the inside back cover.

Word list

Jobs
accountant _____
doctor _____
electrician _____
engineer _____
factory worker _____
hairdresser _____
journalist _____
lawyer _____
office worker _____
photographer _____
postal worker _____
salesclerk _____
teacher _____

Vocabulary

Jobs

1 Order the letters to form jobs.

o d r c o t   _doctor_

1 o r f t y a c   e k r o r w   _____

2 t c a n t o u n a c   _____

3 n r e n i g e e   _____

4 n t e l e c c r i i a   _____

5 j o t s i r a n l u   _____

6 s a t p o l   k e o r r w   _____

7 i d h a r r r e e s s   _____

8 c t a e e r h   _____

9 y e a r l w   _____

10 c o e f f i   r e k o r w   _____

2 Write two jobs for each category.

They wear a uniform:
    postal worker   _doctor_

1 They work in an office:
_____   _____

2 They work with people:
_____   _____

3 They help people:
_____   _____

4 They ask questions:
_____   _____

Grammar

Simple past: Regular verbs
Affirmative

3 Write sentences.

I / listen to / my new CD yesterday.
I listened to my new CD yesterday.

1 Jade / wash / her hair last night.
_____

2 Mom / talk / to my math teacher yesterday.
_____

3 I / ask / the teacher a question.
_____

4 They / open / a new library last summer.
_____

5 He / wait / for the bus for half an hour.
_____

Simple past: Regular verbs
Spelling variations

4 Complete the chart with the simple past form of the verbs.

Base form	Simple past
stop	_stopped_
cry	1 _____
live	2 _____
prefer	3 _____
try	4 _____
study	5 _____
use	6 _____
plan	7 _____

5 Complete the sentences with the simple past form of the verbs in parentheses.

Jack **studied** (study) English in New York last summer.

1 We _____ (live) in a big house on Margate Street when I was a child.

2 They _____ (arrive) at the airport at 6 p.m.

3 I _____ (try) to send you an e-mail but there was a problem with my computer.

4 Sophie _____ (cry) at the end of the movie.

5 Mark _____ (visit) his grandparents last Sunday.

6 We _____ (watch) an episode of *Heroes*.

7 They _____ (play) basketball for three hours.

Simple past: Irregular verbs

6 Find seven more simple past verbs.

C	T	H	W	B	E	F	G	B	C
A	H	H	S	V	D	R	A	N	K
W	O	R	E	A	R	K	H	N	M
K	U	S	N	S	A	I	D	H	W
J	G	L	T	B	V	N	K	J	R
F	H	Y	O	D	K	A	Q	K	O
B	T	R	G	A	V	E	P	L	T
U	U	B	O	U	G	H	T	S	E

7 Complete the sentences with the simple past form of the verbs in the box.

> come drink give go have
> read put run ~~see~~ take write

I <u>saw</u> the movie *Bolt* on DVD last night.

1 All my friends _____ to my birthday party.
2 We were late for school so we _____ to the bus stop.
3 Our teacher _____ us lots of homework last night.
4 I _____ a sandwich and an apple to school for my lunch.
5 I _____ the poster of L.A. Lakers on my bedroom wall.
6 I _____ breakfast and then I _____ to school.
7 I _____ lots of water before the game.
8 I _____ all the questions in the test carefully and then I _____ the answers.

8 Choose the correct answers. (You can check your answers at the bottom of the page.) Then write sentences.

The American War of Independence (start)
ⓐ 1775   b 1762   c 1783.

The American War of Independence started in 1775.

1 Christopher Columbus (discover)
  a Australia   b Antarctica   c America
2 Brazil (win) the Football World Cup in
  a 1954 and 1958   b 1958 and 1962
  c 1962 and 1966
3 The first American president (be)
  a J F Kennedy   b George Washington
  c George Bush
4 The first Olympic Games (take) place in
  a Mexico   b England   c Greece
5 In 1624 Dutch colonists (buy) Manhattan island from Native Indians for
  a $24   b $240   c $24,000

9 Use the correct form of the verbs in parentheses to complete the sentences. Use the time expressions to help you decide which tense to use.

I usually <u>wake up</u> at 7 a.m., but yesterday I <u>woke up</u> at 9 a.m. (wake up / wake up)
We often <u>go</u> to the movies on Sundays. Last Sunday we <u>saw</u> the movie *Enchanted*. (go / see)

Solutions to exercise 8
1c 2b 3b 4c 5a

1 I usually _____ my homework after dinner, but yesterday I _____ it in the afternoon. (do / do)
2 I _____ to the new Kooks CD at the moment. My friend _____ it to me for my birthday. (listen / give)
3 My brother _____ a new computer game last week. He _____ it at the moment. (buy / play)
4 I never _____ fast food but I _____ a hamburger last night. (eat / eat).
5 He _____ the e-mail last Friday. I _____ a reply now. (send / write).
6 We usually _____ by bus to the center, but yesterday we _____ a taxi. (go / take)

Round-up

10 Complete the text with the words in the box. Use the correct forms of the simple past.

> arrive be come ~~drive~~ eat get
> leave look see walk want watch

I'm on vacation with my family in San Diego at the moment. We live in Phoenix and we <u>drove</u> here. We ¹ _____ home after breakfast and ² _____ at our hotel in the Gaslamp Quarter in the evening, two days ago. We ³ _____ all tired but my brother ⁴ _____ to see the big ships so we ⁵ _____ to the harbor – it isn't far from our hotel. It was amazing. There were lots of ships and the city ⁶ _____ beautiful at night.
Yesterday, we ⁷ _____ up early and went to Sea World. It was good fun. We ⁸ _____ some amazing animals and fish, and we ⁹ _____ sea lions and dolphins perform. We also saw sharks, but I don't like them.
In the evening, we ¹⁰ _____ back to the Gaslamp Quarter for some food. There were lots of different restaurants. We ¹¹ _____ in a Japanese restaurant because I love sushi. It was a great day and I hope today is fun as well.

W17

Student Book pp.30–33

Apologizing and making excuses

1 **Write the words in the correct order.**

1

David	Mr. / Excuse / Clarke / me
	Excuse me, Mr. Clarke.
Mr. Clarke	Yes, David. What is it?
David	book / today / my / English / I / sorry / have / but / I'm / don't
	1 _____
	_____
Mr. Clarke	Where is it?
David	home / at / it / I / left
	2 _____
Mr. Clarke	Never mind. Work with Naomi.
David	Thanks, Mr. Clarke.

2

Pam	Hi, Sal. Do you have my Red Hot Chili Peppers CD?
Sal	sorry / at / I'm / It's / home / Oh
	3 _____
Pam	It doesn't matter. Give it to me on Monday.

2 **Complete the dialogue with the expressions in the box.**

> It doesn't matter
> I'm using it at the moment
> I can borrow Anthony's dictionary
> I have basketball practice   ~~What is it?~~
> I left my jacket in the library

1 Janet	Excuse me, Mrs. Rose.
Mrs. Rose	Yes, Janet. **What is it?**
Janet	I'm sorry, but ¹ _____.
Mrs. Rose	Don't worry. You can go and get it now.
Janet	Thank you, Mrs. Rose.
2 Megan	Can you come shopping with me this afternoon, Hannah?
Hannah	I'm sorry, I can't. ² _____ _____
Megan	³ _____. We can go tomorrow afternoon.
3 Ken	Can I borrow your dictionary, Helen?
Helen	I'm sorry but ⁴ _____ _____.
	I'm doing my homework.
Ken	Never mind! ⁵ _____ _____

3 **Apologize and use the prompts to make excuses.**

A Do you have my *Pirates of the Caribbean DVD*?
B (leave / at home)
  I'm really sorry, but I left it at home.

1 A Where were you last night?
  B (go / movie theater)
  _____

2 A Why weren't you at the movie theater at 8 o'clock?
  B (bus / be late)
  _____

3 A Can I borrow your cell phone?
  B (not have / credit / at the moment)
  _____

4 A Can I use the Internet, Dad?
  B (write / e-mail / at the moment)
  _____

5 A You were an hour late for the party!
  B (train / be late)
  _____

6 A Let's go to the movies this evening.
  B (not / have / money)
  _____

4 **Use the instructions to write a dialogue.**

1 A Stop someone politely and ask the time.
  B Apologize and say you don't know because you don't have a watch.

2 A Suggest going bowling this evening.
  B Apologize and say that you have a guitar lesson.
  A Say not to worry and suggest going tomorrow evening.
  B Accept.

3 A Ask your friend why he / she is late.
  B Apologize and say that you took the wrong bus.
  A Tell your friend it doesn't matter. Tell him / her the movie starts at 8:30 and you have the tickets.

4 A Ask your brother if he wants to play a computer game with you.
  B Say you're watching TV at the moment.
  A Ask your brother what he's watching.
  B Say that you're watching a very good movie but it's nearly finished. Say that you can play the computer game after the movie.

Reading

THE GREAT FIRE OF CHICAGO

The Great Fire of Chicago began on October 8th, 1871. It started in or near Mrs. O'Leary's barn. The O'Learys were a poor family. Mrs. O'Leary kept cows in a barn and sold their milk to her neighbors. Historians don't know exactly how the fire began, but newspapers at the time said that one of Mrs. O'Leary's cows knocked over a lamp and started the fire.

The fire spread quickly. It was a hot day and there was a strong wind. There were only 200 firefighters in the city of Chicago and some of them went to the wrong address. They tried to put out the fire but failed. People ran through the streets. They went to Lake Michigan and other safe parts of the city. Some people returned to their houses and tried to save their things. They carried furniture, books, clothes, and pets through the streets.

The fire did terrible damage to the city. It destroyed 17,000 buildings. 100,000 people lost their homes. It burned all night and the next day. In the evening, it started raining and the fire stopped. People from all over the country sent money, clothes, and food and the people of Chicago started rebuilding their city.

1 Are the sentences true or false? Correct the false statements.

1 The Great Fire of Chicago started in 1781.
<u>False. It started in 1871.</u>

2 It started in Mrs. O'Leary's house.
_____

3 It started raining on the day the fire began.
_____

4 There were 2,000 firefighters in Chicago.
_____

5 Some of the firefighters went to the wrong address.
_____

6 The fire destroyed 17,000 homes.
_____

7 The fire burned for four days and four nights.
_____

8 People from all over the world sent money to help rebuild the city.
_____

Writing

2 Imagine you were there when the Great Fire of Chicago happened. Complete the questionnaire and then write a paragraph about your experience.

Where were you when the fire started?
_____

Who were you with?
_____

Describe what you saw.
_____

Describe what you heard.
_____

Describe what personal possessions you saved.
_____

Describe where you went / where you lived after the fire.
_____

Describe what you and your family plan to do next.
_____

4 Grammar rules

Simple past
Negative

Full forms	Short forms
I **did not work**	I **didn't work**
you **did not work**	you **didn't work**
he **did not work**	he **didn't work**
she **did not work**	she **didn't work**
it **did not work**	it **didn't work**
we **did not work**	we **didn't work**
you **did not work**	you **didn't work**
they **did not work**	they **didn't work**

subject + *did not* / *didn't* + base form
I **did not** / **didn't** study.

1 **We make the negative form of the simple past with *did not* + base form of the verb.**
I **did not play** with Tom.

2 **We make short forms with *did* + *n't*. We use short forms more often than full forms.**
You **didn't call** your cousin.

3 **The simple past negative is the same for all people. It doesn't change.**
I **didn't study** for the exam yesterday.
He **didn't play** his guitar at the concert.
We **didn't listen** to the words of the song.

4 **We form the simple past in the same way with regular and irregular verbs.**
Regular verbs
They **watched** the soccer game on TV.
They **didn't watch** the soccer game on TV.

Irregular verbs
We **saw** the movie yesterday.
We **didn't see** the movie yesterday.
NOT We ~~didn't saw~~ the movie yesterday.

Simple past
Interrogative and short answers

Interrogative	Short answers	
	Affirmative	**Negative**
Did I work?	Yes, you **did**.	No, you **didn't**.
Did you work?	Yes, I **did**.	No, I **didn't**.
Did he work?	Yes, he **did**.	No, he **didn't**.
Did she work?	Yes, she **did**.	No, she **didn't**.
Did it work?	Yes, it **did**.	No, it **didn't**.
Did we work?	Yes, you **did**.	No, you **didn't**.
Did you work?	Yes, we **did**.	No, we **didn't**.
Did they work?	Yes, they **did**.	No, they **didn't**.

***Did* + subject + base form?**
Did you work?
Yes + personal pronoun + did.
No + personal pronoun + didn't.
Yes, I did.   No, I didn't.

1 **We make the interrogative form of the simple present with *Did* + base form of the verb.**
Did she / we / they play basketball?

2 **We make short answers with *Yes* / *No* + subject pronoun + *did* / *didn't***
Did you buy a DVD yesterday?
Yes, I did. / No, I didn't.

4 **We form the simple past interrogative in the same way with regular and irregular verbs.**
Regular verbs
Did the boys **clean** their bedroom yesterday?
Yes, they **did**. / **No**, they **didn't**.

Irregular verbs
Did they **win** the competition?
NOT Did ~~they won~~?
Yes, they **did**. / **No**, they **didn't**.

Question words + Simple past

Question word	Simple past
What	did you do yesterday?
When	did they arrive in London?
Where	did they go?
What time	did she have lunch?

1 Question word + *did* + subject + base form of the verb?

Why did you call mom?
What time did you **send** the e-mail?
When did the movie **start**?

Summary

Simple past
be

Affirmative	Negative
I / he / she / it **was**	I / he / she / it **wasn't**
we / you / they **were**	we / you / they **weren't**

Interrogative	
Was I / he / she / it?	**Were** we / you / they?

Short answers	
Affirmative	Negative
Yes, I / he / she / it **was**.	**No**, I / he / she / it **wasn't**.
Yes, we / you / they **were**.	**No**, we / you / they **weren't**.

Regular verbs

Affirmative	
Subject + base form of the verb + **-ed**	
play**ed**	watch**ed**

Negative	
Subject + **didn't** + base form of the verb	
... **didn't play**	... **didn't watch**

Interrogative	
Did + subject + base form of the verb?	
Did you **play**?	**Did** you **watch**?

Short answers	
Affirmative	Negative
Yes, + subject pronoun + **did**.	**No**, + subject pronoun + **didn't**.

Irregular verbs

Affirmative	
Subject + simple past form of the verb	
went	**saw**

Negative	
Subject + **didn't** + base form of the verb	
... **didn't go**	... **didn't see**

Interrogative	
Did + subject + base form of the verb?	
Did you **go**?	**Did** you **see**?

Short answers	
Affirmative	Negative
Yes, + subject pronoun + **did**.	**No**, + subject pronoun + **didn't**.

Word list

Movies
action movie _____
animated movie _____
comedy _____
fantasy movie _____

horror movie _____
love story _____
science fiction movie _____
thriller _____

Exercises

Vocabulary

Movies

1 Complete the kinds of movies with
a, e, i, o, or *u.*

1 c _ m _ d y
2 t h r _ l l _ r
3 _ n _ m _ t _ d
4 h _ r r _ r
5 f _ n t _ s y
6 l _ v _
7 sc _ _ _ _ _ f _ _ _ _ _ _
8 _ c t _ _ n

Which types are usually followed by *movie*?

an <u>action</u> movie

an ¹ _____ movie
a ² _____ movie
a ³ _____ movie
a ⁴ _____ movie

2 Read the movie plots. Then choose the
correct answers.

> It's Halloween and people are celebrating.
> But one vampire isn't wearing a costume …
>
> comedy / (horror movie)
>
> 1 Three children enter a parallel universe
> with unicorns, dragons, and other magical
> animals …
>
> **fantasy movie / love story**
>
> 2 Mickey Mouse has a problem.
> It's Christmas and he doesn't have a
> present for his girlfriend Minnie …
>
> **action movie / animated movie**
>
> 3 A young boy lives in a distant galaxy in the
> year 2565. He travels in space with his
> father and meets some friendly aliens …
>
> **horror movie / science fiction movie**
>
> 4 A poor English boy wins a ticket to travel
> to America. On the ship he meets a rich girl
> and they fall in love …
>
> **love story / action movie**
>
> 5 A police officer investigates the
> assassination of a famous politician. He
> wants to find the assassin. But the assassin
> wants to find the police officer, too …
>
> **comedy / thriller**

Grammar

Simple past
Negative

3 Write the sentences in the correct order.

didn't / read / Tom / on the weekend / a book
<u>Tom didn't read a book on the weekend.</u>
Jill / yesterday / didn't / a DVD / watch
<u>Jill didn't watch a DVD yesterday.</u>

1 have / a pizza / didn't / They
_____
2 Chinese restaurant / didn't / Tom / go / to the
_____
3 do / Anna and Leo / didn't / their homework
_____
4 a bus / Jill / catch / didn't
_____
5 Tom / a T-shirt / buy / didn't
_____

4 Complete the sentences with the simple past
negative form of the verbs in the box.

do   go   ~~like~~   play   send   watch

I <u>didn't like</u> the movie very much.
1 Mark _____ tennis on the weekend.
2 You _____ this homework very well.
3 We _____ shopping yesterday.
4 I _____ Kate a text message.
5 They _____ TV last night.

5 What did you do on the weekend? Check (✔)
or cross (✘) the activity. Write sentences with
information about you.

go swimming   ✔
I went swimming.
read a book   ✘
I didn't read a book.

1 have a pizza   ☐
2 watch a movie   ☐
3 send an e-mail   ☐
4 play soccer   ☐
5 visit a friend   ☐

4

Simple past
Interrogative and short answers

6 **Choose the correct answers.**

Did you (wear) / wore your new skirt to the party?
No, I didn't. I wore my jeans.

1 Did the movie finish late?
Yes, it **finished** / **did**. It finished at 11 p.m.
2 Did they go to Tampa on the weekend?
No, they **didn't** / **not went**. They went to Miami.
3 **Do you bought** / **Did you buy** some chocolates for Maria?
No, I didn't. I bought some flowers.
4 Did Jane see Robert yesterday?
Yes, she **did** / **saw**. She saw him yesterday afternoon.
5 Did Nick **got** / **get** any presents on his birthday?
Yes, he did. He got four or five.
6 Did you like the movie?
No, I **didn't like** / **didn't**.

7 **Write questions. Answer the questions with information for you.**

you / study English / last year?
Did you study English last year?
Yes, I did. / No, I didn't.

1 you / have / a birthday party?
_____
_____

2 you / take / the bus to school today?
_____
_____

3 you / take / a shower this morning?
_____
_____

4 you / see / your cousins on the weekend?
_____
_____

5 you / watch / a movie on the weekend?
_____
_____

Question words + Simple past

8 **Write the questions in the correct order. Then write the answers.**

9th GRADE TRIP TO WASHINGTON

Bus leaves: 8:15 a.m.
Morning: Visit The White House
Lunch: Eat packed lunch in President's Park
Afternoon: National Museum of American History

Bus arrives back at school: 6:00 p.m.

go / did / the students / where?
Where did the students go?
They went to Washington.

1 leave / time / the bus / what / did / ?
2 did / in the morning / they / do / what / ?
3 have / they / did / lunch / where / ?
4 visit / when / the Museum of American History / they / did / ?
5 did / what / arrive / the bus / time / back at school / ?

Round-up

9 **Complete the dialogue with the words in the box.**

~~Did you~~   Did you   Did you   didn't see
took   you do   we did   we didn't   went

Dad _Did you_ have a good trip to Hollywood?
Mark Yes, I did. I loved it.
Dad What did [1] _____ there?
Mark We did a lot of different things. We went on a tour of Paramount Studios and saw how they make movies. It was really interesting.
Dad Did you see any actors?
Mark No, [2] _____. We wanted to see some actors, but we [3] _____ any.
Dad [4] _____ stay there all day?
Mark No, we didn't, but we visited the Walk of Fame and Ben [5] _____ a photo of me next to Johnny Depp's star. It was amazing.
Dad [6] _____ do anything else?
Mark Yes, we did. We [7] _____ to a movie theater and watched a movie.
Dad You watched a movie!
Mark Er, yes, [8] _____. It was in an old movie theater.

Buying a movie ticket

1 Put the dialogue in the correct order.

A Thanks. ☐

A OK. Can I have one adult ticket and two children's tickets, please? ☐

B It's at 8 p.m. ☐

A Which screen is it, please? ☐

A What time is the next showing of *Up*, please? ☐ 1

B It's screen 7. ☐

B OK, that's $25. ☐

A Here you are. ☐

A In the center, please. ☐

B Yes, sure. Where do you want to sit? ☐

B $30, thank you. Here are your tickets and $5 change. ☐

2 Use the information to write a dialogue.

1 A one adult ticket / two children's tickets / for *Alvin Superstar*?

   Can I have one adult ticket and two children's tickets for "Alvin Superstar", please?

   B yes / $28

   _____

2 A What time / next screening / *Into the Wild*?

   _____

   B 9:30

   _____

3 A Which screen / *The Spiderwick Chronicles* / on?

   _____

   B screen 7.

   _____

3 Use the instructions to write a dialogue.

You   Ask the time of the next screening of *Dragon Hunters*.

   What time is the next screening of "Dragon Hunters", please?

Clerk   Tells you the time (6:30).
   1 _____

You   Ask for one adult ticket and three children's tickets.
   2 _____

Clerk   Replies positively and tells you the total price ($26).
   3 _____

You   Give the ticket clerk $40.
   4 _____

Clerk   Gives you your tickets and your change.
   5 _____

You   Ask which screen it is on.
   6 _____

Clerk   Answers your question (screen 5).
   7 _____

You   Thank the clerk and say goodbye.
   8 _____

4 Look at the movie theater information and then use the instructions to write short dialogues.

Movie Screening Times

Screen

Nim's Island
2:00 p.m.   6:00 p.m.   9:00 p.m.   **1**

Water Horse
2:30 p.m.   7:00 p.m.   9:30 p.m.   **2**

Happily n'Ever After
2:00 p.m.   6:30 p.m.   **3**

Admission prices
Adults $12   Over 60s £5   Under 10s $10

1 You're with your grandad. He's 68 years old. You want to watch *Nim's Island*. Buy two tickets for the 9 p.m. screening. Pay with the exact money. The clerk tells you which screen the movie is on.

   A Can we [1] _____
      for the 9 p.m. screening of [2] _____?
   B Yes, sure. That's [3] _____.
      _____
   A Thank you. *Nim's Island* is [4] _____.

2 You're with an adult and a child of nine years old. You want to watch *Happily N'Ever After*. Buy three tickets and pay with a $50 note. The ticket clerk gives you your tickets and change.

   A Can I _____
   B _____
   A _____
   B _____
   A Thank you. Goodbye.

Reading

A Multimedia Superhero

He's almost 200 years old, but he has the body of a young man. He speaks ten languages and he's an expert in martial arts. He's part human, part animal, and part machine. Who is he? He's Wolverine – one of the world's favorite superheroes.

Readers first saw Wolverine in 1974 in a Marvel comic book. In the beginning, he was a minor character but readers liked him and they wanted more. Wolverine appeared again in the comic book series. These were science fiction stories about a group of mutants with superhuman powers, the X-Men. Wolverine was one of their leaders.

In 1992 Wolverine and the X-Men moved to TV. They appeared in the animated TV series *X-Men*. It was one of the big hit shows of that time.

In 2000 popular Australian actor Hugh Jackman played the part of Wolverine in *X-Men – The Movie*. In the movie a mutant called Magneto wants to start a war with humans but Wolverine and the other X-Men stop him. There were two more X-Men movies but people wanted to see more of Wolverine. In 2009 the movie *X-Men Origins: Wolverine* appeared in movie theaters around the world. The movie explains the mysteries of Wolverine's past and how he became a mutant.

Today Wolverine appears in comic books, TV series, video games, and movies. He is a multimedia superhero.

1 Answer the questions

1 How old is Wolverine?

_____

2 How many languages does he speak?

_____

3 When did Wolverine first appear in a comic book?

_____

4 Which comic book series was Wolverine in?

_____

5 What is an X-Man?

_____

6 When did *X-Men* become a TV series?

_____

7 Who played the part of Wolverine in the X-Men movies?

_____

8 What is the movie *X-Men Origins: Wolverine* about?

_____

☆ star factfile ☆

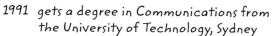

Date of birth:
October 12ᵗʰ, 1968

Place of birth:
Sydney, Australia

1991	gets a degree in Communications from the University of Technology, Sydney
1992	completes a drama course in the Actors' Centre in Sydney
1994	graduates from The Western Australian Academy of Performing Arts
1995	stars in an Australian soap opera where he meets his wife, actress Deborah Lee Furness
1998	appears in the musical "Oklahoma!" in London
2000	plays the part of Wolverine in "X-Men – The Movie"
2004	stars in the movie "Van Helsing"
2009	presents the Academy Awards Ceremony in Los Angeles

Writing

2 Use the information in the factfile to write a paragraph about actor Hugh Jackman.

Hugh Jackman was born in Sydney, Australia on October 12ᵗʰ, 1968. In 1991, he got a ...

3 Imagine you are interviewing Hugh Jackman. Prepare five questions to ask him about his life.

5 Grammar rules

Present progressive for future

1 We use the present progressive to talk about something that is happening now.
Tom**'s** doing his homework at the moment.

2 We also use the present progressive to talk about future plans.
We**'re doing** a math test tomorrow.

3 When we use the present progressive for future, we need to say when.
I'm meeting my friend **on Friday afternoon**.

Affirmative		
I	**'m (am)**	playing
you	**'re (are)**	playing
he	**'s (is)**	playing
she	**'s (is)**	playing
it	**'s (is)**	playing
we	**'re (are)**	playing
you	**'re (are)**	playing
they	**'re (are)**	playing

Subject + | am ('m)
is ('s)
are ('re) | + verb + -ing

4 We make the present progressive with the present simple of **be** + base form of the verb + **-ing**.
I**'m** play**ing**. They**'re** eat**ing**.

5 For most verbs we add **-ing** to the base form.

6 However, there are some spelling variations:
– verbs ending in **-e** – drop the **-e** and add **-ing**.
have ⟶ hav**ing**
– short verbs ending in a vowel plus a consonant – double the final consonant and add **-ing**.
sit ⟶ sit**ting**

Negative		
I	**'m not (am not)**	playing
you	**aren't (are not)**	playing
he / she / it	**isn't (is not)**	playing
we / you / they	**aren't (are not)**	playing

Subject + | am not ('m not)
is not (isn't)
are not (aren't) | + verb + -ing

7 We make the negative form of the present progressive with **be** + **not** + base form of the verb + **-ing**.
I**'m not** listening.
We **aren't** speaking.

Interrogative		
Am	I	playing?
Are	you	playing?
Is	he	playing?
Is	she	playing?
Is	it	playing?
Are	we	playing?
Are	you	playing?
Are	they	playing?

Am
Is | + subject + verb + -ing?
Are

8 We make the interrogative form of the present progressive with **be** + subject + base form of the verb + **-ing**.

Short answers	
Affirmative	**Negative**
Yes, you **are**.	No, you **aren't**.
Yes, I **am**.	No, I**'m not**.
Yes, he **is**.	No, he **isn't**.
Yes, she **is**.	No, she **isn't**.
Yes, it **is**.	No, it **isn't**.
Yes, you **are**.	No, you **aren't**.
Yes, we **are**.	No, we **aren't**.
Yes, they **are**.	No, they **aren't**.

Am
Is | + subject + base form of the verb + -ing
Are
Yes, | + subject pronoun + *am / is / are.*
No, | + subject pronoun + *'m not / isn't / aren't.*

• We make short answers of the present progressive with **Yes,** + subject pronoun + **be** or **No,** + subject pronoun + **be**.
Are you working? **Yes, I am.**
Is she tidying her room? **No, she isn't.**

Future time expressions

1 We use the present progressive for future with these time expressions:

- *this ... morning / afternoon / evening tonight*
  They're leaving **this afternoon**.
- *tomorrow ... morning / afternoon / evening / night*
  We're going to London **tomorrow night**.
- *next ... Friday / week / month / summer / year*
  They're moving house **next week**.
- *At + the time*
  at 12 o'clock, at midnight, at 3 p.m.
  We're meeting Jennifer **at 4 p.m.**
- *At + longer period of time*
  at Christmas, at Easter
  We're going on holiday **at Easter**.
- *On + the day or the date*
  on 3rd August, on my birthday, on Monday, on Christmas Day, on the weekends
  I'm having a big party **on my birthday**.
- *In + the month, season, year*
  in August, in the summer, in 2012
  He's moving to Australia **in 2012**.

Question words + Present progressive

1 **We make the interrogative form of the present progressive with question words + *be* + subject + verb + ing.**

Question words	+	am is are	+ subject + verb + -ing?

What are you eating?
Why are you crying?

How long...? + take

1 **We use *How long* + *take* to ask about length of time.**
How long does it **take** you to walk to school?
It **takes** me fifteen minutes.

2 **We can use *How long* + *take* with or without the subject pronoun *you*.**
How long does **it take** to drive to Manchester?
It takes four hours.
How long does **it take you** to have breakfast?
It takes me about 20 minutes.

3 **We can answer the question *How long* + *take* with these expressions:**
about (five) minutes
(ten) minutes
a quarter of an hour
half an hour
three quarters of an hour
an hour
an hour and a half
two and a half hours

Word list

Transportation
airplane _____
bike _____
boat _____
bus _____
car _____
ferry _____
helicopter _____
motorcycle _____
subway _____
taxi _____
train _____
truck _____

5 Exercises

Vocabulary

Transportation

1 Match and write the forms of transportation.

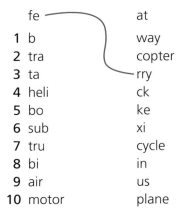

	fe	at
1	b	way
2	tra	copter
3	ta	rry
4	heli	ck
5	bo	ke
6	sub	xi
7	tru	cycle
8	bi	in
9	air	us
10	motor	plane

2 Choose the correct answers.

You get on and get off a (bus) / car / taxi.

1 You get into and get out of a **motorcycle / boat / car**.
2 An **airplane / truck / train** lands and takes off.
3 You drive a **bike / car / ferry**.
4 You ride a **bike / truck / car**.
5 You catch a **train / bike / car**.
6 You take a **car / bus / bike**.

Grammar

Present progressive for future

3 Complete the affirmative (✔) or negative (✗) sentences or questions (**?**).

<u>Is Jade cleaning</u> (Jade / clean) her bedroom tomorrow. (**?**)

1 _____ (I / go) to the dentist next month. (✔)
2 _____ (we / have) a math test next Friday? (**?**)
3 _____ (dad / cook) dinner on the weekend? (**?**)
4 _____ (I / go) to Andy's party on Saturday. (✗)
5 _____ (Jo / visit) her cousins at Easter. (✗).
6 _____ (Mom / drive) me to school tomorrow. (✔)

4 Use the notes to write sentences with the present progressive for future. Add prepositions of time where necessary.

I / have / party / 19ᵗʰ July
I'm having a party on July 19ᵗʰ.

1 We / go / to Mexico / January
2 The party / start / 8 o'clock.
3 I / have / a party with my friends / next Friday
4 My older brother / come / home / Easter
5 We / finish / history project / tomorrow afternoon
6 They / visit / their grandparents / Christmas day

5 Read the information and complete the dialogue.

English Language Summer School

Student's name:	Jae Hee Lee
Nationality:	South Korean
Age:	15
Departure:	January 23ʳᵈ, Seoul Airport
Flight number:	KF234
Destination:	Manly, Sydney
Accommodation:	Australian family: Mr. & Mrs. Abbott
Length of stay:	2 weeks

Thank you!

You	Where are you going on vacation next summer?
Jae Hee	<u>I'm going to Australia.</u>
You	What are you doing there?
Jae Hee	1 _____
You	How are you traveling there?
Jae Hee	2 _____
You	Where are you staying?
Jae Hee	3 _____
You	Who are you staying with?
Jae Hee	4 _____
You	How long are you staying?
Jae Hee	5 _____

Future time expressions

6 Write the future time expressions in chronological order.

> at 9 p.m. tonight   next month
> next week   ~~next year~~   on Friday
> ~~this afternoon~~   this weekend
> tomorrow morning

1 this afternoon
2 _____
3 _____
4 _____
5 _____
6 _____
7 _____
8 next year

How long ...? + take

7 Use the information to write questions and answers.

> go from Belo Horizonte to Vitoria by train = 12 hours
> How long does it take to go from Belo Horizonte to Vitoria by train?
> It takes 12 hours.

1 fly to the moon by spacecraft = 3 days
_____
_____

2 drive from Montreal to Ottawa = about two hours
_____
_____

3 walk one kilometer on foot = 12 minutes
_____
_____

4 fly from London, England to Sydney, Australia = 22 hours
_____
_____

5 Travel from England to France by ferry = 90 minutes
_____
_____

Round-up

8 Read the clues and write the transportation.

You can call for this. taxi

1 You can take this from city to city. Japan has a famous one that is very fast.
_____

2 This can fly a long way. _____

3 You can get this in the city. It is a small train. New York, Tokyo, and Seoul have this.
_____

4 This goes in the water from place to place.
_____

5 A lot of people go to school on this.
_____

6 A lot of people drive this. _____

9 Complete the dialogue with the correct form of the verbs in the box.

> ~~come~~   drive   fly   go   go
> make   stay   take   take   they / arrive
> they / stay   you / do

Sara   Why are you so happy, Jenny?

Jenny   My cousins from Canada **are coming** tomorrow. They [1] _____ from Vancouver. I'm really excited.

Sara   That's great news. How old are they?

Jenny   Ross is fifteen and Kath is fourteen.

Sara   What time [2] _____?

Jenny   At about 5 p.m., I think. Dad and I [3] _____ to the airport to meet them when they land.

Sara   How long [4] _____?

Jenny   For two weeks with us. Then they [5] _____ a train and they [6] _____ with our grandparents for a week.

Sara   How long [7] _____ to go from here to your grandparents?

Jenny   It takes an hour and a half. Mom [8] _____ a lot of food because Ross eats a lot!

Sara   What [9] _____ with them when they are here?

Jenny   We [10] _____ to Yosemite National Park. We [11] _____ biking and camping. I can't wait!

5 Communication

Making arrangements

1 Complete the dialogue with the phrases below.

> ~~Are you free~~   Let's do   How about
> Why don't   See you then   a great idea
> At what time

Sarah   Hi, Olivia. **Are you free** tomorrow evening?

Olivia   No, I'm not. I'm seeing Kate tomorrow, but I'm free on Tuesday evening.

Sarah   Great. ¹_____ something together on Tuesday, then.

Olivia   Good idea. What do you want to do?

Sarah   ²_____ going to the movies?

Olivia   There aren't any good movies on at the moment. ³_____ we go bowling, instead?

Sarah   That's ⁴_____. Let's meet in front of my house.

Olivia   OK. ⁵_____? How long does it take to get there?

Sarah   It takes about 30 minutes. Is seven thirty OK?

Olivia   Yes, that's fine. ⁶_____.

2 Put the phrases in the correct order. Then write the dialogue.

A Let's go to the swimming pool. ☐
B After lunch. At half past two. Is that OK? ☐
A Let's do something together. ☐ 1
B Let's meet at the entrance to the park. ☐
A That's a great idea. Where shall we meet? ☐
B I don't like swimming. Why don't we go rollerblading, instead? ☐
A Yes, that's fine. ☐ 9
B Good idea. What shall we do? ☐
A At what time? ☐

A Let's do something together.
B _____
A _____
B _____
   _____
A _____
B _____
A _____
B _____
A Yes, that's fine.

3 Use the information to complete the dialogue. Use the dialogue in exercise 1 as a model

ProAudio Concerts Presents
RAZORLIGHT
Saturday, 7th November
At the Odyssey Arena
Concert starts 8 p.m.   Ⓡ

(ticket stub) ProAudio Concerts Presents RAZORLIGHT Saturday, 7th November At the Odyssey Arena

A Let's go to the Razorlight Concert on Saturday.
B That's a great idea. Where ¹_____?
A ²_____ at the Odyssey Arena.
B At what time?
A It starts at 8 o'clock. so ³_____ 6:30.

4 Use the information to write the dialogue.

> ♫ **Music, food, dancing!** ♫
> *Celebrate at the end-of-year School Party on Friday, July 4ᵗʰ in the School Hall.*
> The party starts at 7 p.m.
> Entrance fee: $5

A _____
B _____
A _____
B _____
A _____
B _____
A _____

5 Read the instructions and write a dialogue.

1 You invite your friend to go ice-skating with you on Saturday afternoon. Your friend accepts. He / she loves ice-skating. You arrange a time and place to meet.

2 You invite your friend to watch a DVD at your house. Your friend refuses because he / she has a test the next day. You invite your friend to come on the weekend. He / She agrees. You arrange a time.

Reading

1 Read the article quickly and find out where the people live.

John _____

Emma _____

Anabeli _____

How do you go to school?

The majority of students go to school by bus, by car, or on foot. But for some students the journey to school is very different.

John lives in the U.K. on an island 25 km from the north coast of Scotland. His island is very small and only 37 people live there. Every morning he rides his bike to the port and takes the ferry. The journey takes about an hour. He usually plays with his games console. He also listens to music, reads, or does his homework.

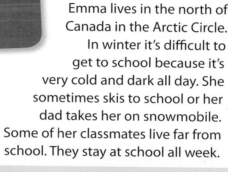

Emma lives in the north of Canada in the Arctic Circle. In winter it's difficult to get to school because it's very cold and dark all day. She sometimes skis to school or her dad takes her on snowmobile. Some of her classmates live far from school. They stay at school all week.

Anabeli lives on the small island Unije off the coast of Croatia. She loves going to school because she goes by airplane! She says, "School starts next week so my brother and I are flying to another island to go to school next Tuesday and Thursday. We only go twice a week!"

2 Answer the questions.

1 How does John get to his school?

_____

2 How long does his journey take?

_____

3 How does Emma get to school in winter?

_____

4 What does Anabeli use to get to school?

_____

5 How often does she go to school?

_____

Writing

3 Answer the questions and then use your answers to write a short paragraph about your journey to school.

- Where do you live? (town, country, village, city)
- How far away is your school?
- How do you get to school?
- How long does your school journey take?
- What time do you leave the house?
- Who do you travel with? (alone, with friends, family …)
- What do you do on the journey? (listen to music, chat to friends …)
- Do you like / dislike your journey. Why?

I live in Chota in the north of Peru. My school isn't near my house.

6 Grammar rules

Countable / Uncountable nouns

Countable		Uncountable
Singular	**Plural**	**Only singular**
an orange	two oranges	water
a book	two books	rice

1 We use countable nouns to describe things we can count. Countable nouns can be singular or plural.

a pen ⟶ five pens

2 We can use *a / an* with singular countable nouns in positive and negative sentences.

I have **a** book but I don't have **a** pen.

3 We use uncountable nouns to describe things we cannot count. Uncountable nouns can only be singular.

bread NOT ~~a bread, two breads~~

some / any

Uncountable	Countable
Affirmative	
There is **some** water.	There are **some** eggs.
Negative	
There isn't **any** water.	There aren't **any** eggs.
Interrogative	
Is there **any** water?	Are there **any** eggs?

1 We can use *some* with plural countable nouns and uncountable nouns. We use *some* in positive sentences.

We have **some** milk.
I bought **some** apples in the market.

2 We use *any* with plural countable nouns and uncountable nouns. We use *any*:

– **in negative sentences**
I didn't buy **any** bananas.
I didn't buy **any** milk.

– **in questions**
Did you buy **any** bananas?
Did you buy **any** milk?

3 We use *some* with polite requests and offers, *Can I have ...?* or *Would you like ...?*

Can I have some juice, please?
Would you like some cheese?

a lot of / much / many

Uncountable	Countable
Affirmative	
There is **a lot of** cheese.	There are **a lot of** eggs.
Negative	
There isn't **much** cheese.	There aren't **many** eggs.
Interrogative	
Is there **much** cheese?	Are there **many** eggs?

1 *A lot of*, *much* and *many* are all expressions which mean "a large quantity".

2 We use *a lot of* in positive sentences. We use *a lot of* with plural countable and uncountable nouns.

There are **a lot of** students in my school.
I bought **a lot of** paper.

3 We use *much* in negative sentences and questions. We use *much* with uncountable nouns.

I don't have **much** time.
Do you do **much** sport at school?

4 We use *many* in negative sentences and questions. We use *many* with plural countable nouns.

I don't have **many** DVDs.
Do you have **many** friends?

How much...? / How many...?

Uncountable	Countable
How much cheese is there?	**How many** eggs are there?

1 We use *How much...?* and *How many...?* to ask about quantities.

2 We use *How much...?* to ask about uncountable nouns.
How much coffee do we have?

3 We use *How many...?* to ask about plural countable nouns.
How many children are there?

a little / a few

Uncountable	Countable
There is **a little** cheese.	There are **a few** eggs.

1 *A little* and *a few* are expressions which mean "a small quantity".

2 We use *a little* with uncountable nouns.
I have **a little** sugar in my coffee.

3 *A little* means the same as *not much*.
There's **a little** milk in the cup.
There **isn't much** milk in the cup.

4 We use *a few* with plural countable nouns.
There are **a few** CDs on the table.

5 *A few* means the same as *not many*.
I know **a few** foreign students.
I **don't** know **many** foreign students.

Summary chart:
Expressions of quantity

We can use these with countable nouns:
a / an, some / any, How many...?, a lot of, many, a few.

We can use these with uncountable nouns:
some / any, How much...?, a lot of, much, a little.

Word list

Food and drink
apple _____
beef _____
bread _____
carrot _____
cheese _____
cookie _____
egg _____
mango _____
milk _____
orange juice _____
potato _____
rice _____
salmon _____
tomato _____
tomato sauce _____
tuna _____
vegetables _____
water _____
yogurt _____

Meat
beef _____
chicken _____
duck _____
ham _____
lamb _____
mutton _____
pork _____

Vocabulary

Food and drink

1 Look at the pictures and complete the puzzle. What are the mystery words?

1   2   3

4   5   6

7   8   9

10   11

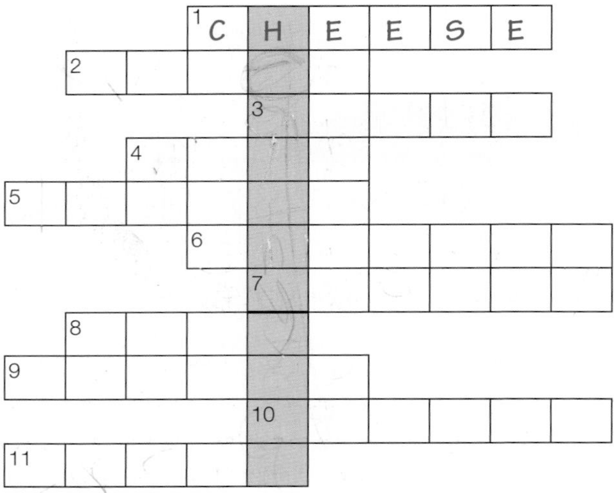

	1 C	H	E	E	S	E

(crossword grid with entries 2–11)

Grammar

Countable / Uncountable nouns

2 Complete the chart with the words in the box.

> bread   carrot   cheese   cookie   egg
> ~~mango~~   orange juice   rice   tomato   tuna

Countable	Uncountable
mango	5 _____
1 _____	6 _____
2 _____	7 _____
3 _____	8 _____
4 _____	9 _____

some / any

3 Complete the sentences with *a*, *an*, or *some* or *any*.

I don't have _a_ pen.
There's _an_ apple on the table.
I eat _some_ vegetables every day.
There isn't _any_ cheese in the refrigerator.

1 I put _____ tomato sauce on my chips.
2 I had _____ cookie before I left home.
3 I bought _____ new clothes yesterday.
4 Is there _____ orange juice for breakfast?
5 Mom gave me _____ sandwich.
6 I can't see _____ eggs in cupboard.

4 What ingredients are in tomato sauce? Look at the label and write affirmative and negative sentences with *some* and *any*.

TOMATO SAUCE

Ingredients: tomatoes, onions, olive oil, salt, sugar, vinegar, black pepper

tomatoes: _There are some tomatoes._

1 water: _____
2 onions: _____
3 sugar: _____
4 carrots: _____
5 butter: _____
6 vinegar: _____

a lot of / much / many

5 Write affirmative (✔) or negative (✗) sentences or questions (?) using *a lot of*, *much*, or *many*.

You / oil / salad (✗)
You don't put much oil on your salad!
students (✔)
There are a lot of students here.

1 I / eat / eggs (✔)
2 I / play / sports (✔)
3 we / have / time (✗)
4 you / have / homework (?)
5 Sue / have / cousins (✗)
6 Louise / eat / meat (?)

How much ...? / How many ...?

6 Choose the correct question words. Answer the questions with true information.

How much / How many questions are there in this exercise?
There are five questions.

1 How much / **How many** students are there in your class?

_____

2 How much / **How many** cousins do you have?

_____

3 **How much** / How many fruit do you eat every day?

_____

4 How much / **How many** people are there in your family?

_____

5 **How much** / How many money do you spend on CDs a week?

_____

a little / a few

7 Look at the pictures. Write questions and two answers for each question. Use *How much ...?* and *How many ...?* and *not much, not many, a little,* and *a few.*

How much milk is there?
There isn't much milk.
There's a little milk.

 1 _____

 2 _____

 3 _____

 4 _____

 5 _____

Round-up

8 Complete the table with the words in the box.

apple   carrot   cheese   chocolate
cookie   lamb   ~~mango~~   orange juice
pork   potato   water   yogurt

1 Fruit: *mango*, _____
2 Vegetables: _____, _____
3 Meat: _____, _____
4 Dairy products: _____, _____
5 Sweets: _____, _____
6 Drinks: _____, _____

9 Look at the picture. Read the dialogue and choose the correct answers.

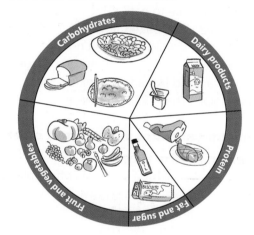

Q Do we need meat for a healthy diet?
A Well, there is **a lot of** / much protein in meat and we need [1] **some** / any protein every day. But [2] **some** / any people, vegetarians for example, don't eat [3] some / **any** meat. There is [4] **a lot of** / much protein in other foods, for example, fish, eggs, and nuts.
Q [5] **How much** / How many fruit do we need every day?
A We need [6] much / **a lot of** fruit and vegetables. Doctors recommend five portions a day. They are good snacks because they have [7] **a lot of** / much minerals and vitamins but they don't have [8] much / **many** calories.
Q [9] How many / **How much** milk do we need every day?
A Well, milk has calcium and we need [10] any / **some** calcium in our diet. Cheese also has calcium, but dairy foods have [11] much / **a lot of** fat, and a healthy diet doesn't have [12] **much** / many fat.

Ordering food and drink

1 Complete the dialogue with the words in the box.

> ~~How can I help~~ I'd like I'll have
> Large, please like to drink
> with tuna Yes, please

Server <u>How can I help</u> you?
Mark ¹_____ a chicken sandwich, please.
Server OK. What would you ²_____?
Mark ³_____ a soda.
Server Large or small?
Mark ⁴_____.
Server OK. And what about you? What would you like to eat?
Susan I'd like a baked potato ⁵_____.
Server OK. Would you like a drink?
Susan ⁶_____. I'll have an orange juice and I'd like a few cookies, too.
Server OK. That's $15.75 please.

2 Write the sentences in the correct order.

1 Server Small or large? ☐
   Boy Yes. I'll have a cup of coffee, please. ☐
   Boy I'd like a tuna sandwich, please. ☐
   Server Can I help you? ☐1
   Server OK. And, would you like a drink? ☐
   Boy Small, please. ☐

2 Girl I'd like a ham pizza, please. ☐
   Girl No, thanks. ☐
   Server Would you like chips with that? ☐
   Server What would you like to eat? ☐
   Girl I'll have a small soda, please. ☐
   Server And, what would you like to drink? ☐

3 Complete the dialogue with the words in the box.

> drink eat for have like
> like 'll please thanks What ~~would~~

Server What <u>would</u> you like to ¹_____?
Tom I'd ²_____ a cheese sandwich, please.
Server Would you ³_____ some chips?
Tom No, ⁴_____.
Server OK. ⁵_____ would you like to ⁶_____?
Tom I'll ⁷_____ a small orange juice, ⁸_____.
Server Fine. And ⁹_____ you?
Kelly I don't want any food, but I ¹⁰_____ have a large glass of soda, please.

4 Look at the picture and complete the dialogue.

1

Server What would you like to eat?
You I'll <u>have</u> a ¹_____.
Server Would you like a drink?
You Yes, please. I'd ²_____.

2

Server What would you like to eat?
You I'd ³_____, please.
Server Would you like a drink?
You ⁴_____.

3

Server What would you like to eat?
You I'll ⁵_____ tuna
     ⁶_____, please.
Server Would you like a drink?
You ⁷_____. I'd like a glass
     ⁸_____.

5 Look at the menu on page 64 of the Student Book. Use the instructions to write the dialogue.

Server Asks if he can help you.
     1_____
You Order something to eat.
     2_____
Server Asks you if you'd like a drink.
     3_____
You Say what drink you'd like.
     4_____
Server Asks you if you'd like a large or small drink.
     5_____
You Reply for you.
     6_____

Skills

Reading

What's on the menu?

In the U.S., students have lunch at school. They can bring a lunch box from home or they can buy a hot lunch at school. A few years ago, school meals weren't very healthy. They often had a lot of food with fat, for example hamburgers and French fries. Today, some schools are changing their menus. They offer a lot of healthy food, too, for example fruit and vegetables.

But what do students have for lunch in other countries? Let's find out!

Japan

❝We can buy lunch at school or eat food from home. A lot of students take their food to school in a special lunch box called a *bento*. These have four or five sections: for rice, fish or meat, vegetables and fruit. The menu in our school canteen is quite healthy. It often includes sushi and other Japanese dishes.❞

Kiyoshi

Australia

❝Our school has a traffic light system to help the students choose healthy food. Food with a red label has a lot of fat, sugar and salt. An orange label means that the food is quite healthy and green means that the food is very healthy. I don't eat much food with red labels. I try to only eat food with orange or green labels.❞

Ellie

1 Read the text. Answer the questions.

1 Where do American students have their lunch?

2 What options do they have for lunch?

3 What is a *bento*?

4 Where can you find *bento* boxes?

5 What type of food is often on the school lunch menu at Kiyoshi's school?

6 How does Ellie's school help students choose healthy food?

7 What does a red label on food mean?

Writing

2 Write a paragraph about lunchtime at your school. Use these questions to help you.

- What time do you have lunch?
- Where do you have lunch?
- What type of lunch do you have? (school lunch, a lunch box from home, lunch at home)
- What type of lunch do your classmates usually have?
- Is your lunch healthy or unhealthy?

Comparative adjectives

1 We use comparative adjectives to talk about differences between two things or people.
Tom **is** tall**er than** his brother.

2 We use *than* after the adjective and before the second thing or person.
The Amazon is longer **than** the Thames.
São Paulo is bigger **than** New York.

Short adjectives

Short Adjectives		
Adjective		**Comparative**
fast	**+ -er**	fast**er (than)**
old		old**er (than)**
small		small**er (than)**
large	**+ -r**	larg**er (than)**
nice		nic**er (than)**
big	double the	big**ger (than)**
sad	consonant **+ -er**	sad**der (than)**

1 With short adjectives we add **-er**.
long + **-er** ⟶ long**er**
slow + **-er** ⟶ slow**er**
strong + **-er** ⟶ strong**er**

2 With adjectives that end with **-e** we add **-r**.
close + **-r** ⟶ clos**er**
late + **-r** ⟶ lat**er**
wide + **-r** ⟶ wid**er**

3 With short adjectives ending in a vowel plus a consonant we double the final consonant and add **-er**.
thin + **ner** ⟶ thin**ner**
big + **ger** ⟶ big**ger**
hot + **ter** ⟶ hot**ter**

Adjectives ending with -y		
Adjective		**Comparative**
happy	**-y and + -ier**	happ**ier (than)**
funny		funn**ier (than)**

4 With adjectives ending **-y** we drop **-y** and add **-ier**.
tidy ⟶ tid**ier**
heavy ⟶ heav**ier**
easy ⟶ eas**ier**

Long adjectives

Long Adjectives		
Adjective		**Comparative**
important	**more +**	**more** important **(than)**
boring	adjective	**more** boring **(than)**
interesting		**more** interesting **(than)**

1 With long adjectives we put *more* + adjective + *than*.
Math is **more difficult than** geography.
Action movies are **more exciting than** love stories.

2 Some adjectives of two syllables follow the same rules as short adjectives.
clever ⟶ clever**er**
narrow ⟶ narrow**er**
quiet ⟶ quiet**er**
simple ⟶ simpl**er**
Cats are **cleverer** than dogs.

3 With some two-syllable adjectives, the short adjective and long adjective patterns are both correct (adding **-er** or *more*). You can check the correct comparative form of an adjective in a dictionary.
common ⟶ common**er (than)**
⟶ **more** common **(than)**

Irregular adjectives

Irregular adjectives	
Adjective	**Comparative**
good	**better (than)**
bad	**worse (than)**
far	**further (than)**

- Some adjectives are irregular. You need to learn them.
Tim is **better** than Tom at volleyball.
My school is **further** than yours.

as ... as

as ... as				
Tom isn't	as	old	as	Ashley.
CDs aren't	as	expensive	as	DVDs.
Is the movie	as	exciting	as	the book?

We put *as* before and after the adjective.
We use *as ... as* to say how two things or people are the same.
You are **as** tall **as** my brother.
My brother is **as** tall **as** you.

We use *not as ... as* to say how two things or people are not the same.
English is**n't as** difficult **as** Japanese.
My hair is**n't as** long **as** yours.
The Blue Lake Hotel is**n't as** cheap **as** The Gardenia Hotel.
Walking is**n't as** quick **as** taking the bus.
Johnny Depp's new movie is**n't as** funny **as** *The Pirates of the Caribbean*.

less ... than

1 We can use *less* before the adjective.
Books are **less interesting than** movies.

2 *Less ... than* means the same as *not as ... as*.
A bus **is less** expensive **than** a taxi.
A bus **isn't as** expensive **as** a taxi.

3 We use *not as ... as* more often than we use *less ... than*.

Word list

Geography
continent _____
country _____
desert _____
island _____
lake _____
mountain _____
ocean _____
river _____
sea _____
volcano _____

Exercises

Geography

1 Reorder to find eight more geography words.

e a s	s _ea_
1 s l a d i n	i_____
2 v r e i r	r_____
3 a t n m u n o i	m_____
4 e n o a c	o_____
5 t e r s e d	d_____
6 n i t n e o c n t	c_____
7 k e l a	l_____
8 c o o v l a n	v_____

2 Complete the sentences. Use words from exercise 1.

The Rio Negro is a very long _river_.

1 Bermuda is an _____.
2 Mount Everest is a _____ in the Himalayas.
3 Mount Tungurahua in Ecuador is an active _____.
4 Loch Ness is a famous Scottish _____.
5 The Caribbean _____ is to the north of Colombia.
6 At night, it's cold in the Sahara _____.
7 Charles A. Lindbergh was the first man to fly solo across the Atlantic _____.
8 Did you know that Australia is a country and a _____?

Comparative adjectives
Short adjectives

3 Complete the chart.

Adjective	Comparative
tall	_taller_ (than)
long	1 _____ (than)
happy	2 _____ (than)
hot	3 _____ (than)
funny	4 _____ (than)
slow	5 _____ (than)
large	6 _____ (than)
old	7 _____ (than)
nice	8 _____ (than)

4 Write comparative sentences. Use the adjectives from exercise 3.

My sister runs 100 m in 13.5 seconds. I take 11.6 seconds.
My sister's slower than me.

1 I'm 14 years old. My brother is 12 years old.
_____
2 Today, it's 28°C. Yesterday, it was 22°C.
_____
3 Cartoons are funny. Documentaries are boring.
_____
4 My sister is 1.30 m. I'm 1.55 m.
_____
5 The blue T-shirt is large. The black T-shirt is small.
_____
6 The book has a sad ending. The movie has a happy ending.
_____
7 The Nile is 6,650 km. The Amazon is 6,400 km.
_____
8 Mr. York is nice. Mrs. Hardwick gives us lots of homework.
_____

Long adjectives

5 Make comparisons using the adjectives in parentheses.

Snowboarding is _more exciting than_ skiing. (exciting)

1 Train tickets are _____ bus tickets. (expensive)
2 Gwyneth Paltrow is _____ Sandra Bullock. (famous)
3 Dolphins are _____ dogs. (intelligent)
4 Motorcycles are _____ cars. (dangerous)
5 Linkin Park are _____ Metallica. (popular)
6 Do you think history is _____ science? (boring)

Irregular adjectives

6 Complete the chart.

Irregular adjective	Comparative
good	1 _____ (than)
bad	2 _____ (than)
far	3 _____ (than)

7 Complete the dialogue with the comparative form of the adjectives in parentheses.

Hannah Let's go for something to eat before we go to the movies.

Luke Good idea. Why don't we go to Fast Pizza?

Daniel No, I hate Fast Pizza. Let's go to Ben's Burgers instead. The food is **better** (good) there.

Luke I don't like Ben's Burgers. Fast Pizza is ¹ _____ (cheap) and the atmosphere is ² _____ (relaxed). The people are ³ _____ (friendly), too.

Daniel But it's always full. It's ⁴ _____ (easy) to get a table at Ben's Burgers.

Luke Ben's Burgers is ⁵ _____ (far) from the movie theater. Fast Pizza is very near the movie theater.

Hannah I have an idea! Let's go to Moulin Rouge Café. The food is ⁶ _____ (good) than Fast Pizza's and it's ⁷ _____ (near) the movie theater than Ben's Burgers!

as ... as

8 Write sentences about these famous people using as ... as and the adjectives in parentheses. You can use your own ideas.

Paulo Coelho / J.K.Rowling (old)
J.K.Rowling isn't as old as Paulo Coelho.
Gerry Scotti / Will Smith (famous)
Gerry Scotti isn't as famous as Will Smith.

1 Adam Sandler / Owen Wilson (funny)

_____

2 Matt Damon / Johnny Depp (famous)

_____

3 Fanny Lu / Paulina Rubio (good looking)

_____

4 Robinho / Ji-Sung Park (talented)

_____

5 Anne Hathaway / Keira Knightley (tall)

_____

less ... than

9 Rewrite the sentences using less ... than.

London is more interesting than Paris.
<u>Paris is less interesting than London.</u>

1 Portuguese is more difficult than English.

_____

2 Basketball is more popular than baseball.

_____

3 Concert tickets are more expensive than movie tickets.

_____

4 Science is more important than English.

_____

5 Kylie Minogue is more famous than Dannii Minogue.

_____

10 Rewrite your answers to exercise 9 using not as ... as.

Paris is less interesting than London.
Paris isn't as interesting as London.

Round-up

11 Choose the correct answers.

North America and South America are two very different continents but they are both **interesting as /** **as interesting as** each other. North America and South America both have mountains, deserts, lakes, and famous rivers. The Patagonian Desert in South America is ¹ **bigger / bigger than** the deserts in North America, but it isn't ² **less hot as / as hot as** Death Valley. The Atacama Desert in South America is ³ **dryer / drier** than the Patagonian Desert. And what about water? Which continent has the ⁴ **larger / more large** lake? Is it Lake Superior in North America or Lake Maracaibo in Venezuela? Lake Superior is bigger, but it isn't ⁵ **as deeper as / as deep as** Argentino Lake in Argentina. In terms of rivers, the Amazon is ⁶ **longer / more long** than The Mississippi (but only by 117 km)! Finally, which continent has the ⁷ **higher / more higher** mountain? The answer is South America with the Cerro Aconcagua in Argentina. In fact, the only mountains higher than Cerro Aconcagua are in Asia, but it is still 2,654 m ⁸ **less high than / less higher than** Mount Everest. Maybe Mount Everest is ⁹ **more famous / famouser**, though.

Asking for tourist information

1 **Complete the dialogue with the phrases below.**

> does it open   as fast as   Where is it
> can I get   ~~Can I help~~   as many
> How much

Assistant Good morning. **Can I help** you?

Paula Yes, please. I want to visit the Empire State Building. ¹_____ are the tickets?

Assistant They're $20 for adults and $14 for children.

Paula What time ²_____?

Assistant It's open from 8 a.m. to 2 a.m. every day. There aren't ³_____ people there at 1 p.m. as at 11 p.m.

Paula ⁴_____?

Assistant It's on 5ᵗʰ Avenue. Between 33ʳᵈ and 34ᵗʰ Streets.

Paula How ⁵_____ there?

Assistant You can take the subway to 34ᵗʰ Street or get a bus. The bus is ⁶_____ the subway and you can see the city. Or you can walk. It takes about 45 minutes and it's cheaper than the bus or the subway!

Paula Thanks.

Assistant You're welcome. Have a nice day!

2 **Match the questions and answers.**

1 Can I help you?   c
2 Where is it?   ☐
3 How much are the tickets?   ☐
4 Is there a students' discount?   ☐
5 How can I get there?   ☐
6 What time does it open?   ☐

a It's on 5ᵗʰ Avenue, opposite 81ˢᵗ Street.
b It's open from 9:30 a.m. to 5:30 p.m. every day.
c Yes, please. I want to go on the Metropolitan Museum of Art.
d You can take the subway or the bus.
e They're $20 for adults and it's free for children.
f Yes, there is. It's $10 for students.

3 **Imagine that you work in a tourist information office. Look at the information and answer the questions.**

The Statue of Liberty

Location: Liberty Island, New York
Opening times: Open every day, except Christmas Day 8:30 a.m. – 6:15 p.m.
Tickets: Adults: $12 / Children $5 / Over 60s $10. Extra $3 to go into the Crown of the statue
Transportation: Ferry from Battery Park

You Hello. **Can I help you?**

Tourist Yes, please. I want to visit The Statue of Liberty. Where is it, please?

You ¹_____

Tourist How can I get there?

You ²_____

Tourist How much are the tickets?

You ³_____

Tourist Is there a students' discount?

You ⁴_____

Tourist What time does it open and close?

You ⁵_____

Tourist That's great. Thanks very much.

4 **Imagine that you're a tourist in Australia. Use the information below and write a dialogue in a tourist information office. Use the dialogue in exercise 3 as a model.**

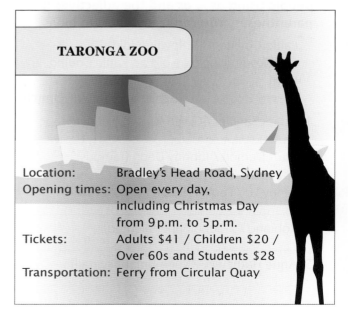

TARONGA ZOO

Location: Bradley's Head Road, Sydney
Opening times: Open every day, including Christmas Day from 9 p.m. to 5 p.m.
Tickets: Adults $41 / Children $20 / Over 60s and Students $28
Transportation: Ferry from Circular Quay

Reading

1 Read the text about Bahia quickly and find the name of:

The capital city   ¹ _____

A national park   ² _____

An archipelago   ³ _____

Welcome to Beautiful Bahia

The state of Bahia is in the northeast of Brazil. It's the perfect place for a vacation! Here are some of the things you can see and do there.

Salvador – Capital of Happiness

Salvador is the capital city of the region. It's smaller than Sao Paulo or Rio but some people say it's more Brazilian. The old part of the town has beautiful, colorful houses and monuments from the 17th century. The carnival in Salvador is spectacular. It takes place in February and over 200 groups take part in the parades. The carnival party lasts for seven days and seven nights!

A Natural Paradise

The Chapada Diamantina National Park is in the center of Bahia. It's a beautiful region of mountains, rivers, waterfalls, and natural swimming pools and it's less populated than the coast. It's perfect for active tourists. There are lots of things to do like walking, mountain biking, swimming, and snorkelling.

To the Ocean

Whale watching is a popular activity in the Abrolhos archipelago off the south coast of Bahia. Thousands of tourists visit the region from July through November when the whales migrate there. It's also famous for its colorful, exotic fish and spectacular coral formations.

2 Answer the questions

1 Where is Bahia?

_____

2 What is the capital city of the region?

_____

3 What can tourists see in the old part of Salvador?

_____

4 How long does the carnival party last?

_____

5 Where is the Chapada Diamantina National Park?

_____

6 What can tourists do in the park?

_____

7 Where is the Abrolhos archipelago?

_____

8 What is it famous for?

_____

Writing

3 Write a tourist brochure for a region in your country. Use the reading text as a model and include the following information ...

- location
- geography
- cities
- places to visit
- things to do

Welcome to ... It's the perfect place for a vacation ...

8 Grammar rules

Superlative adjectives

1 **We use superlative adjectives to compare three or more things or people.**
Tom is **the tallest** boy in the school.

2 **We often follow superlative adjectives + noun with *in* or *of*.**
- *in* + most phrases: *in* Colombia, *in* my school, *in* my family.
The Amazon is the longest river **in** the world.
Luke is the fastest player **in** the team.
- *of* + other phrases: *of* my life, *of* the year.
It was the longest vacation **of** my life.

Short adjectives

Short adjectives		
Adjective		**Superlative**
fast	**the** + adjective + **-est**	**the** fast**est**
high		**the** high**est**
tall		**the** tall**est**
large	**the** + adjective + **-st**	**the** larg**est**
safe		**the** saf**est**
big	**the** + adjective double the final consonant + **-est**	**the** big**gest**
sad		**the** sad**dest**

1 **With short adjectives we add *-est*.**
long + -est ⟶ **the** long**est**
slow + -est ⟶ **the** slow**est**
strong + -est ⟶ **the** strong**est**

2 **With adjectives that end with *-e* we add *-st*.**
close + -st ⟶ **the** clos**est**
wide + -st ⟶ **the** wid**est**
nice + -st ⟶ **the** lat**est**

3 **With short adjectives ending in a vowel plus a consonant we double the final consonant and add *-est*.**
thin + **nest** ⟶ **the** thin**nest**
big + **gest** ⟶ **the** big**gest**
hot + **test** ⟶ **the** hot**test**

Adjectives ending with **-y**		
Adjective		**Superlative**
happy	**the** + adjective -y + **-iest**	**the** happ**iest**
funny		**the** funn**iest**

4 **With adjectives ending -y we drop *-y* and add *-iest*.**
tidy ⟶ **the** tid**iest**
heavy ⟶ **the** heav**iest**
easy ⟶ **the** eas**iest**

Long adjectives

Long adjectives		
Adjective		**Superlative**
important	**the most** + adjective	**the most** important
boring		**the most** boring
interesting		**the most** interesting

1 **With long adjectives we put *the most* + adjective.**
Tim is **the most intelligent** boy in my class.
That is **the most boring** book in the world.

2 **Some adjectives of two syllables follow the same rules as short adjectives.**
clever   the clever**est**
narrow   the narrow**est**
quiet   the quiet**est**
simple   the simpl**est**
Parliament Street is **the narrowest** street in England.

3 **With some two-syllable adjectives, the short adjective and long adjective patterns are both correct (adding *-est* or *most*). You can check the correct superlative form of an adjective in a dictionary.**

Irregular adjectives

Irregular adjectives	
Adjective	Superlative
good	the best
bad	the worst
far	the furthest / the farthest

- Some adjectives are irregular. You need to learn them.
  That was **the worst** day of my life.

Comparative / Superlative

1 We can use the comparative to compare two people or things. We can compare them in three different ways:
   - **in a positive way**
     Jean **is prettier than** her sisters.
   - **in a negative way**
     Jean is **less pretty than** her cousins.
     Jean is**n't as pretty as** her cousins.
   - **to say things are the same**
     Jean is **as pretty as** her mom.

2 We can use the superlative to compare three or more people or things.

3 We can compare in two different ways:
   - **in a positive way**
     He is **the most interesting** person in town.
   - **in a negative way**
     He is **the least interesting** person in town.

the least

Adjective		Superlative
difficult	the least +	the least difficult
dangerous	adjective	the least dangerous
interesting		the least interesting

1 We use **the least** to say that something is less than the others. **The least** is the superlative form of less.

2 We put **the least** before the adjective.
   I have got **the least difficult** job in the office.

3 We often follow **the least** + noun with:
   - **in** + most phrases: **in** Vietnam, **in** my school, **in** my family
     This is the least interesting place **in** Mexico.
     He was the least nervous **in** the team.
   - **of** + other phrases: **of** my life, **of** the year
     Tom is the least interesting **of** my friends.

Word list

Feelings and emotions
angry _____
annoyed _____
bored _____
confident _____
embarrassed _____
excited _____
fed up _____
frightened _____
happy _____
nervous _____
proud _____
sad _____

Vocabulary

Feelings and emotions

1 Match the sentence halves.

1 I'm fed up!   [d]
2 I'm really sad because
3 He's very nervous. He
4 I'm really proud because
5 Sue's very annoyed with you.
6 Tom was really happy
7 Jo was embarrassed when
8 Sam was really frightened when

a She thinks that you broke her MP3 player.
b when he passed the exam.
c he saw the shark in the water.
d ~~I've got a test tomorrow and I wanted to go to the beach today.~~
e she fell asleep at school. Everyone laughed at her.
f has an exam tomorrow.
g my best friend's moving to another town.
h I got the best marks in the test.

Grammar

Superlative adjectives
Short adjectives

2 Complete the sentences with the superlative form of the adjectives in parentheses.

Nina is the **fastest** (fast) runner in the team. She can run 100 m in eleven seconds.

1 This is the _____ (pretty) beach on the island.
2 Simon is the _____ (tall) person in my family.
3 Thanks for the present, Rona! You're the _____ (nice) person in my class.
4 Ali's the _____ (clever) student in our class.
5 Why do I have to carry the _____ (heavy) bag?
6 My _____ (old) brother is at university.
7 When my dog died, it was the _____ (sad) day of my life.

3 Read the information and write sentences.

Superheroes *CTTV Thurs 7:30 p.m.*
Three champions, ten sports, and only one Superhero! Meet this week's competitors.

Tim Lanton, 20, is the Chicago Blue Caps $20 million star basketball player.
2.1m tall   85 kg

Jess Trinman, 25, was an Olympic 100 m runner, so she's really fast.
1.8 m tall   72 kg

Marius Dubrovski, 24, is a boxing world champion, and he's very strong!
1.7 m tall   95 kg

heavy   <u>Marius is the heaviest.</u>
1 tall   _____
2 fast   _____
3 short   _____
4 old   _____
5 light   _____
6 strong   _____
7 young   _____

Long and irregular adjectives

4 Complete the dialogue with the correct form of the adjectives in parentheses.

Mel   What song are you listening to?
Lucy   It's "Umbrella" by Rhianna. It's **the most popular** (popular) song from her album. Who's your favorite singer, Mel?
Mel   Justin Timberlake. I love him. I think he's the ¹ _____ (good) singer and the ² _____ (fashionable) star in America.
Lucy   Yeah, he's OK.
Mel   OK! He's one of the ³ _____ (famous) singers in the world!

5 Complete the information about the computer games with the correct form of the adjectives in parentheses.

★★★★★ excellent	★★★★ very good	★★★ good	★★ OK	★ bad

Zanderhan
Can you escape from the castle of Zanderhan?   **$12.⁹⁹**   ☆☆☆ ☆☆

Our opinion
This is ¹ _____ (popular) game in the stores at the moment, and we can see why. It's one of ² _____ (good) and ³ _____ (exciting) games around. It's also the ⁴ _____ (cheap) new game this week. Excellent!

Dark Star
Meet scary aliens in this science-fiction adventure.   **$14.⁹⁹**   ☆☆

Our opinion
Dark Star takes you to the ⁵ _____ (far) star in our galaxy. You meet ⁶ _____ (angry) aliens in the galaxy, but it isn't very exciting. We think it's ⁷ _____ (bad) new game this week.

6 Write sentences that are true for you.

exciting / video game
I think the most exciting video game is "The Lost Ark".

1 popular / singer in my country
2 bad / school subject
3 funny / cartoon character

Comparative / Superlative

7 Complete the sentences with the comparative or superlative form of the adjectives in the parentheses.

Sue always smiles. I think she's **the happiest** (happy) person in my class.

1 My cell phone is _____ (good) than yours.
2 It was _____ (embarrassing) day of my life!
3 Don't read that book. This one is _____ (interesting).
4 I know it's _____ (expensive) bike in the shop, but I want it.
5 My brother's _____ (strong) than you.
6 I think she's _____ (funny) comedian on TV.

the least

8 Complete the sentences with *the least* and the words in the box.

difficult   ~~dangerous~~   confident
popular   expensive

Whale sharks are **the least dangerous**.

1 I hate speaking in French lessons because I'm _____ person in my class.
2 She's _____ actress in Hollywood. Nobody likes her.
3 I'm good at drawing so art is _____ school subject for me.
4 Let's have a pizza. It's _____ thing on the menu.

Round-up

9 Choose the correct answers.

Do you think you can eat a lot? How about the (largest) / most large hamburger in the world? It weighs 55.79 kg and costs $379. Or, are you faster than Peter Dowdeswell? He is the world's ¹ **fastest / most fast** hamburger eater. He ate 21 hamburgers in 9 minutes 42 seconds.

Do you get bored quickly? We hope not because the ² **longest / longgest** lesson took 73 hours and 37 minutes. It was a lesson on English grammar.

Do you feel short? The world's ³ **talest / tallest** man was Robert Wadlow. He was 2.72 m tall.

Would you like some new shoes? What about the shoes from the movie *The Wizard of Oz*? They are the ⁴ **expensivest / most expensive** shoes at $165,000!

Are you frightened of animals? Look out for poison arrow frogs because they are the ⁵ **most dangerous / dangerousest** animals in the world.

Making a phone call

1 Complete the dialogue with the words in the box.

> for you   ~~Is this Meg~~
> leave a message   My number is
> return my call   speak with   Who's calling

1

A Hello.

B Hi! It's Becky. <u>Is this Meg</u>?

A No, it isn't. It's her sister. Meg isn't here at the moment. She's at her dance class. Do you want to ¹_____?

B Yes, please. Can you ask her to ²_____ before 8 o'clock at the latest? ³_____ 212-555-0911.

A That's 212-555-0911. OK. Bye.

B Bye.

2

A Hello.

B Hello. Can I ⁴_____ Rick, please?

A Yes, certainly. ⁵_____?

B It's Harry, Rick's best friend.

A Oh, hi Harry! Hang on a minute. Rick! It's ⁶_____. It's Harry.

2 Match the questions and answers.

1 Can I speak to John?   [c]

2 Who's calling?   [ ]

3 Does she have your number?   [ ]

4 Is that Liam?   [ ]

5 Do you want to leave a message?   [ ]

a No, she doesn't. It's 537-566-3499.

b Yes, please. Can you tell him I can't come to basketball practice tonight?

~~c Sorry, he isn't here at the moment.~~

d It's Lucy, I'm Mike's friend.

e No, I'm his brother Tom.

3 Use the instructions to complete the dialogue.

Jenny Hello.

Simon Ask if she is Tanya.
       <u>Is this Tanya?</u>

Jenny No, I'm her cousin Jenny.

Simon Say hello and asks where Tanya is.
       ¹_____

Jenny She's in town with her dad.

Simon Ask for her cell number.
       ²_____
       _____

Jenny She didn't take her cell phone. Do you want to leave a message?

Simon Say you can't meet her at the movie theater tonight.
       ³_____

Jenny OK. Do you want her to ring you back?

Simon Say yes, after six o'clock.
       ⁴_____

Jenny Does she know your phone number?

Simon Say no. Give Jenny your phone number.
       ⁵_____

Jenny That's 787-632-1634. OK, bye then, Simon.

Simon Thank her and say goodbye.
       ⁶_____

4 Use the instructions to write dialogues.

1 You want to call Mick, but you don't know his number. Call Mick's brother Tim and ask for his number.

A ¹_____

B ²_____

A ³_____

B ⁴_____

2 You promised to help your friend Kiera with her homework this afternoon, but you aren't very well today. Call Kiera and tell her you can't come to her house.

A ⁵_____

B ⁶_____

A ⁷_____

B ⁸_____

3 Call your teacher. You left your cell phone in the classroom. Does your teacher know where it is?

A ⁹_____

B ¹⁰_____

A ¹¹_____

B ¹²_____

Reading

Welcome to our new Friends of Mount Rushmore website

Visit Mount Rushmore, the most unusual monument in America and see the faces of four of our greatest presidents – George Washington (1732–1799), Thomas Jefferson (1743–1809), Abraham Lincoln (1809–1865), and Theodore Roosevelt (1858–1919). Each face is 18 m high and they're the largest group of sculptures in the world!

The Mount Rushmore sculptures were the idea of a man called Doane Robinson in the early 1900s. The area around Mount Rushmore was very poor and Robinson wanted to attract tourists. At first, he didn't know what to build there, but then the politicians in Washington agreed to create a memorial to four presidents from the first 150 years of U.S. history. But which four? The politicians had a lot of different opinions and, in the end, the sculptor, Gutzon

Borglum, made the final decision. Gutzon Borglum and his son created the Mount Rushmore sculptures between 1927 and 1941. They had about 400 local workers to help them, but it was still was one of the biggest and most difficult construction jobs in U.S. history. It was also one of the most dangerous, but, amazingly, nobody died. Today, the monument is a popular tourist attraction. More than 2 million people visit it every year!

1 Read the text. Answer the questions.

1 Which presidents can you see at the Mount Rushmore monument?
2 What world record do the sculptures have?
3 Who had the idea for the sculptures?
4 What did he want to do?
5 Who created the sculptures?
6 When did they create them?
7 How many people helped them?
8 How many tourists now visit the Mount Rushmore monument every year?

Writing

2 Read the factfile and write a paragraph about the Grand Canyon Skywalk.

3 Write a paragraph about a popular tourist attraction in your country. Use these questions to help you.

- What is it?
- Where is it?
- What can tourists do there?
- What is special about it?

factfile

The Grand Canyon Skywalk

Where is it?

The Grand Canyon, Arizona

What is it?

A glass walkway over the deepest canyon in the world.

How high is it?

1,200 m above the floor of the Grand Canyon.

Who built it?

The Hualapi Native American people (2006)

What can tourists do?

Walk on the glass and look down at the canyon.

What is special about it?

It's the highest walkway in the world and one of the biggest tourist attractions in the south-west of America.

OXFORD
UNIVERSITY PRESS

Great Clarendon Street, Oxford OX2 6DP

Oxford University Press is a department of the University of Oxford.
It furthers the University's objective of excellence in research, scholarship,
and education by publishing worldwide in

Oxford New York

Auckland Cape Town Dar es Salaam Hong Kong Karachi
Kuala Lumpur Madrid Melbourne Mexico City Nairobi
New Delhi Shanghai Taipei Toronto

With offices in

Argentina Austria Brazil Chile Czech Republic France Greece
Guatemala Hungary Italy Japan Poland Portugal Singapore
South Korea Switzerland Thailand Turkey Ukraine Vietnam

OXFORD and OXFORD ENGLISH are registered trade marks of
Oxford University Press in the UK and in certain other countries

© Oxford University Press 2011

The moral rights of the author have been asserted

Database right Oxford University Press (maker)

First published 2011
2015 2014 2013 2012
10 9 8 7 6 5 4

ISBN: 978 0 19 446207 5

Printed in China

This book is printed on paper from certified and well-managed sources.

ACKNOWLEDGEMENTS

Student Book

The authors and publishers would like to thank all the teachers and
schools who have given generously of their time and expertise during the
development of the course.

Special acknowledgement is due to Claire Thacker for the Curriculum extra
lessons.

*The authors and publisher are grateful to those who have given permission to reproduce
the following adaptation of copyright material:* p.58 *Skateboard wizard of Oz* by Nick
Squires, 18 January 2007, Telegraph.co.uk © Telegraph Media Group Limited
2007. Reproduced by permission.

Illustrations by: Adrian Barclay pp.4 (ex 3), 5 (ex 4), 6 (ex 4); Claude Bordeleau
pp.13, 21; Paul Daviz pp.5 (ex 6), 15, 32, 50, 75; Bruno Drummond pp.8 (ex 11),
42, 43, 64; Chuck Gonzales pp.6 (ex 6), 34; Alberto Hoyos pp.5 (ex 5), 7, 12, 56;
Garry Parsons p.14; Alan Rowe pp.7, 54, 62, 93; Fred van Deelen pp.46, 57, 58,
74 76, 82, 88, 97, 98, 99

Commissioned photography by: Chris King pp.10–11, 18–19, 30–31, 38–39, 52–53,
60–61, 72–73, 80–81

*The publisher would like to thank the following for their kind permission to reproduce
photographs:* Alamy pp.4 (Matthew/imagebroker), (Thomas/Israel images), (Tim/
Image Source), (Sara/imagebroker), (Kevin/Image Source), 16 (players/Enigma),
20 (Bob Marley/Pictorial Press Ltd), 22 (Jay-Z/Steven May), 23 (Mozart/Lebrecht
Music and Arts Photo Library), 23 (Hendrix/Pictorial Press Ltd), 27 (Abba/
Pictorial Press Ltd), 33 (girl/Radius Images), 36 (William Shakespeare/Interfoto
Pressebildagentur), 39 (Marie Curie/Mary Evans Picture Library), 40 (Charlie
Chaplin/Photos 12), 44 (*Transformers*/Photos 12), 44 (*Indiana Jones*/Photos 12),
45 (*Night at the Museum*/Photos 12), 84 (girl on phone/Angela Hampton Picture
Library), 86 (Doctors/Tetra Images), 86 (Chinese wedding/Jon Arnold Images
Ltd), 86 (bride/Keith Morris), 92 (orchestra/Ted Foxx), 96 (plantation/Jordi
Cami), 96 (farmer/Simon Rawles); Corbis UK Ltd. pp.4b (Luisa/Radius Images),
4t (Ralph/Monalyn Gracia), 16 (game/Moodboard), 20 (New Jersey Symphony
Orchestra/Saed Hindash/Star Ledger), 22 (Daniela Mercury/Andrew Gombert/
Epa), 23 (Ella Fitzgerald/Derick A. Thomas/Dat's Jazz), 27 (Pavarotti/Ethan
Miller), 31 (Michael Jordan/Jim Bourg/Reuters), 36 (Christopher columbus/
Bettmann), 37 (Washington/The Gallery Collection), 69 (Hard Rock Cafe

sign/Jan Butchofsky-Houser), 89 (Ashley Tisdale/Sara De Boer/Retna Ltd.), 94
(Eadweard Muybridge still/Hulton Deutsch Collection), 98 (Henry Romero/
Reuters); Getty Images pp.31 (Jackie Joyner-Kersee/Don Emmert/AFP), 33 (boy),
51 (Britt Erlanson), 78 (snake/Chris Mattison/Dorling Kindersley); Guinness
World Records 2010 p.90; Holly Allen/Boardfree p.58 (David Cornthwaite);
Image Net p.40 (*Alice in Wonderland*/Disney Enterprises, Inc); iStockphoto pp.4
(USA flag/Claudio Divizia), 4 (Ella), 6 (Edie Layland), 79 (hamster), (guinea pig/
Eric Isselée), 88 (TV/Dmitry Kutlayev), 88 (laptop/Vladimir Boriso), 92 (music/
Arpad Nagy-Bagoly); Kobal Collection pp, 42 (*Goldeneye*/DANJAQ/EON/UA),
42 (*Gone with the Wind*/Selznick/MGM), 42 (*The Empire Strikes Back*/Lucasfilm/
Twentieth Century Fox); Lonely Planet Images p.89 (Daytona Beach/John
Neubauer); Oxford University Press pp.4 (Sue/Westend61), 4 (Laura/Photodisc),
67 (fruit/Photodisc), 70 (burger and fries/Ingram), 78(tarantula/Photodisc);
Photo12.com pp.94 (*King Kong*/Archives du 7eme Art), 94 (Toy Story/Archives
du 7eme Art); Photolibrary Group pp.55 (Age Fotostock), 59 (Robert Harding
Travel), 83 (Amanda Hall/Robert Harding Travel); Press Association Images
pp.12 (Jack Black), 12 (Taylor Swift), 20 (Rihanna/ABACA USA), 24/25 (Bono),
25 (Shakira/Charles Sykes/Associated Press), 28 (Springsteen/Joel Ryan), 35;
Rex Features pp.12 (Felipe Massa/Masatoshi Okauchi), 20 (Pink Floyd), 20
(50 Cent/Action Press), 22 (Nelly Furtado/Ken McKay), 22 (Tokio Hotel/Action
Press), 22 (Katy Perry/Action Press), 22 (30 Seconds to Mars/Freddie Baez), 24/25
(Live Aid), 25 (Justin Timberlake/KPA/Zuma), 27 (Miriam Makeba/AGF s.r.l.),
28 (Elton John/David Dagley), 31 (Ayrton Senna/Brendan Beirne), 31 (Pele/
Mike Webster), 44 (premiere/Sipa Press), 45 (Astroboy/Everett Collection),
48 (Mickey Mouse/SNAP), 89 (Lucy Liu/Amanda Schwab), 89 (Keira Knightley/
Theo Kingma), 90 (barbecue/Sipa Press), 94 (*Snow white and the seven dwarfs*/
SNAP); Ronald Grant Archive pp.40c (*Frankenstein*/Hammer Film Productions),
40 (Shrek), 45 (Coraline); Shutterstock pp.4 (Union Jack/Route66), 4 (Canadian
flag/Adam Golabek), 4 (Japanese flag), 4 (South Korean flag/Michael Roeder),
4 (Brazilian flag); The Fairtrade Foundation pp.96 (produce), 96 (logo); Walker
Books p.66 (Sam Sterne).

Workbook

Illustrations supplied by: Claude Bordeleau/Agent 002 pp.W10, W35(ex9); Fred
Van Deelan pp.W34, W35(ex7), W36; Alberto Hoyos p.W28; Mark Ruffle
pp.W19, W34, W41.

*The publisher would like to thank the following for their kind permission to reproduce
photographs:* Alamy Images pp.W31 (Ferry/South West Images Scotland), W43
(Whale watching boat/blickwinkel), W48 (Girl on phone/Angela Hampton
Picture Library); Aquarius Library p.W25 (*X-Men Origins: Wolverine*/20th
Century Fox); Corbis pp.W47 (Robert Wadlow/Hulton-Deutsch Collection),
Corbis p.W47 (Ruby slippers/Jason Reed/Reuters); Getty Images pp.W4 (Man
wearing glasses/Pando Hall/Photographer's Choice), W7 (Young woman
with book/Ben Bloom/Stone), W7 (Harvard University, Boston/Fraser Hall/
Robert Harding World Imagery), W12 (Singers Shakira and Argenti/AFP), W25
(Marvel comic book/Bloomberg), W31 (Couple on snowmobile/Brian Bailey/
Stone), W31 (Children boarding plane/Laurence Monneret/Riser), W37 (School
cafeteria/Yellow Dog Productions/The Image Bank), W37 (Japanese bento
lunchbox/Iain Masterton/Photographer's Choice), W43 (Pelourinho Square,
Salvador/Mauricio Simonetti/The Image Bank), W43 (Morro do Pai Inacio,
Palmeiras/Eduardo Bagnoli/SambaPhoto); iStockphoto p.W17 (San Diego
and bay); Oxford University Press pp.W11 (Celebrity signing autographs/
Stockbyte), W46 (Boy with basketball/Photodisc), W46 (Smiling woman/
Digital Vision), W46 (Smiling guy/Corbis/Digital Stock), W49 (Mt. Rushmore/
Photodisc); PunchStock p.W49 (Viewing platform overlooking Grand Canyon/
Photographer's Choice); Rex Features pp.W12 (Ibrahim Ferre/Action Press),
W12 (Live Aid Concert/Nils Jorgensen), W12 (Ricky Martin/David Fisher), W25
(Hugh Jackman/Masatoshi Okauchi).